HYDRIOTAPHIA

OR

THE DEATH OF DR BROWNE

*An Epic Farce about Death
and Primitive Capital
Accumulation*

Tony Kushner

BROADWAY PLAY PUBLISHING INC
New York
www.broadwayplaypub.com
info@broadwayplaypub.com

HYDRIOTAPHIA OR THE DEATH OF DR BROWNE
© Copyright 1987, 1997, 1998, 2000 Tony Kushner

All rights reserved. This work is fully protected under the copyright laws of the United States of America. No part of this publication may be photocopied, reproduced, stored in a retrieval system, or transmitted, in any form or by any means, electronic, mechanical, recording, or otherwise, without the prior permission of the publisher. Additional copies of this play are available from the publisher.

Written permission is required for live performance of any sort. This includes readings, cuttings, scenes, and excerpts. For amateur and stock performances, please contact Broadway Play Publishing Inc. For all other rights please contact Joyce Ketay, The Gersh Agency, JKetay@gersh.com.

First Acting Edition: August 2024
I S B N: 978-0-88145-942-5

Book design: Marie Donovan
Page make-up: Adobe InDesign
Typeface: Palatino

Productions	iv
Thanks	v
Sir Thomas Browne and The Restoration	vi
Dramatis Personae	x
Some Thoughs About the Play	xii
Dedication	xvii
HYDRIOTAPHIA OR THE DEATH OF DR BROWNE	1
An Afterword	125

HYDRIOTAPHIA OR THE DEATH OF DR BROWNE received its first production in June 1987 at HOME for Contemporary Theatre and Art in New York City. It was produced by Heat & Light Co., Inc.

The play was subsequently produced by the Graduate Acting Program of N Y U's Tisch School of the Arts in April 1997.

In 1998, HYDRIOTAPHIA OR THE DEATH OF DR. BROWNE received a co-production by the Alley Theatre in Houston, Texas (Gregory Boyd, Artistic Director; Paul R Tetreault, Managing Director), and Berkeley Repertory Theatre in California (Tony Taccone, Artistic Director; Susan Medak, Managing Director).

Thanks to Michael Mayer for waking the play from its long sleep, and to Zelda Fichandler for approving its first production in eleven years. Michael Wilson got it back on its feet and found its soul again. The NYU cast was magnificent, the Berkeley Rep cast was beyond heroic; the original cast performs the play nightly in my heart of hearts. I am very grateful to Stephen Spinella, Jason Butler Harner and Jonathan Hadary, my three Brownes, for their glorious incarnations of the nasty bloated logorrheic old bugger. The staff at Berkeley Rep saved my life, and are the Platonic ideal of a theater staff. Amy Potozkin and Susie Medak graciously endured a lot of anxious phumping from me, and Michael Suenkel, the stage manager, made the impossible seem a routine matter of little regard.

More than anyone else, my deepest thanks, and much love, go to Tony Taccone, who has been over the years a great friend, in every regard a true gentleman of the theater, and a rare hand with a rubber chicken.

SIR THOMAS BROWNE
AND THE RESTORATION

The number of the dead long exceedeth all that shall live. The night of time far surpasseth the day, and who knows when was the Aequinox? Every houre addes unto that current Arithmetique, which scarce stands one moment. And since death must be the *Lucina* of life, and even Pagans could doubt whether thus to live, were to dye. Since our longest Sunne sets at right decensions, and makes but winter arches, and therefore it cannot be long before we lie down in darkness, and have our light in ashes. Since the brother of death daily haunts us with dying *memento's*, and time that grows old it self, bids us hope no long duration: Diuturnity is a dream and a folly of expectation.

Darknesse and light divide the course of time, and oblivion shares with memory a great part even of our living beings; we slightly remember our felicities, and the smartest stroaks of affliction leave but short smart upon us. Sense endureth no extremities, and sorrows destroy us or themselves. To weep into stones are fables. Afflictions induce callosities, miseries are slippery, or fall like snow upon us, which notwithstanding is no unhappy stupidity. To be ignorant of evils to come, and forgetfull of evils past, is a mercifull provision in nature, whereby we digest the mixture of our few and evil dayes, and our delivered senses not lapsing into cutting remembrances, our sorrows are not kept raw by the edge of repetitions.

[from "Hydriotaphia or Urne-Buriall"
—SIR THOMAS BROWNE

Sir Thomas Browne (1605-1682) was a writer of prodigious genius, coiner of an English-language prose style of such voluptuous baroquosity it melts the straight lines and right angles of the Euclidean universe, stretches every assumption of Cartesian logic, and achieves, by means of a remorselessly tortured syntax, something dialectically poised between Rigorous Reason and Ecstatic Delirium; aiming at science and philosophy, his essays achieve vision and poetry instead. Browne's style influenced writers from De Quincey to Melville, and I believe his ornate jeweled swooniness can be discerned as influence in the works of such contemporaries as Michael Ondaatje and Edmund White.

Browne may have been a thoroughly lovely human being; this play is not intended as a portrait of the historical man, any more than it is an accurate portrait of late-mid-seventeenth-century England. If anything, this is a play about the treachery of words, about writing—probably it's better that I let *you* decide what it's about.

Primitive capital accumulation is a term of Karl Marx's and Friedrich Engels's, making reference to the ugly and vital process whereby a nation that is entering the capitalist phase of economic and social relations dislocates its rural populations in the course of a violent land grab by aristocratic and entrepreneurial classes intent on accumulating, by any means necessary, the material resources that provide the bases for mercantile, manufacturing and speculatory fortunes. From the devastation consequent upon such officially sanctioned piracy, an impoverished urban and factory workforce emerges, desperate for wages. Primitive capital accumulation is the nakedly brutal manner in which money was grubbed from people and land, before the camouflaging, cosmeticization, banalization and normalization of such mayhem, before we learned new words for it, like Modernization, Progress, Industrialization—before the invention of Spin.

Shakespeare lived through the tail end of the roughest phase of primitive accumulation in England, and his plays reflect the chaos of the time, their bloodiness, their immense excitement, and the irreconcilable dissonance between Christianity and capitalism, between unstoppered material appetite and Christ's asceticism, His antipathy toward wealth and usury, His preference for the poor. Widespread misery was occasioned by the seizure of common lands, moors and forests, and their transformation into private property. This misery manifested itself chiefly in waves of homeless rural poor descending on the cities, seeking food, shelter, work, and finding less than they needed; in the fiery growth of religious dissidence, religious radicalism and factionalism, challenging the orthodoxy, feeding rivers of ancient class resentment and the explosive pressures generated by a rapidly rising mercantile class rubbing up against a truculent, greedy aristocracy. A social, political revolution in England in the seventeenth century was inevitable.

Sir Thomas Browne and The Restoration

From 1642-1649, England fought two civil wars, ending with the beheading of the disastrous king Charles I and the establishment of a wobbly Parliamentary republic. In 1653 Oliver Cromwell, a personage of spectacular contradictions, noble intentions and a pronounced capacity for barbarism, backed by the army, ascended to an uneasy dictatorship as Lord Protector and Head of State. In 1658 Cromwell died of malaria, and all hope for a real republic ended quickly; in 1660, with the backing of part of the army, the monarchy was restored in the person of Charles II, who one year later dug up Cromwell's grave in Westminster Abbey, hung his corpse in Tyburn and then decapitated it, keeping the head on a pike atop Westminster Hall where it remained till Charles II died.

Sir Thomas Browne lived through this period, a steadfast supporter of the monarchy throughout the civil wars, the Commonwealth and the Protectorate, for which loyalty he was rewarded with a knighthood in 1671. *Hydriotaphia* takes place in an obviously askew version of this postrevolutionary England, after the Restoration of the Old Order Transformed.

In 1664 Browne's testimony, consisting of disinterested theological speculation, helped hang two women accused of witchcraft.

DRAMATIS PERSONAE

SIR THOMAS BROWNE, *a physician and author. He's fifty years old. He is a thin man, but his body is hugely swollen. He is very wealthy and he is dying.*

HIS SOUL, *tiny, beautiful, but a little soiled; it lives behind the headboard of* BROWNE'S *deathbed. It sings beautifully.*

DAME DOROTHY BROWNE, SIR THOMAS'S *wife, forty or forty-five; she's had fourteen children and a very hard life. She is dressed simply but elegantly.*

BABBO, BROWNE'S *nanny when he was a child, and now his cook. She is very old but busy as a little steam engine—not frail, her brain a little dim, and sweet. She chews a stick of cinnamon.*

MACCABBEE, BROWNE'S *amanuensis/servant/laboratory assistant.* MACCABBEE *has the clap and it has eaten away his nose. In his nose's place he wears a brass prophylaxis, like Tycho Brahe did. The brass nose is held in place with ribbon tied around his head.*

DR EMIL SCHADENFREUDE, BROWNE'S *physician, a Hessian doctor living in Norfolk. He speaks with a remarkable German accent. He is dressed in High Restoration style, as if eager to blend in with London society. A pleasant man enjoying life and his work, an enthusiast.*

DR LEVITICUS DOGWATER, BROWNE'S *pastor and his business partner. A Protestant cleric, he dresses elegantly but severely. He is very robust, and he speaks with a stutter.*

Leonard Pumpkin, *the local gravedigger. He is very handsome and very poor, about twenty-five years old. His hands are always filthy filthy filthy.*

The Abbess of X, *née* Alice Browne, Sir Thomas's *sister, presumed drowned but actually living as the Mother Superior of a convent of British ex-pat assassin nuns. She is dressed in a very severe and very elegant (but suitable for action) nun's habit.*

Doña Estrelita, *the wife of the Spanish ambassador to the British court, a former lover of* Browne's. *She is fifty, immensely wealthy and, when not in disguise, her couture is the very zenith of European decadence and beauty. She speaks with a magnificent Spanish accent.*

Sarah, *a ranter woman, homeless, lives in the forest, a witch. She is dressed in rags. Probably in her twenties or thirties, though so begrimed and worn by life it's hard to tell. She is a person of tremendous power.*

Mary, *a ranter, just like* Sarah, *but of a more thoughtful and gentle disposition.*

Ruth, *a ranter, more bellicose than the other two, and the best at ranting.*

Death, *an immensely fat man, green skin, skull showing through scalp, dressed in rotting Stuart-era finery, wrapped, like Marley's ghost, in chains from which dangle ledger books and counting boxes. He resembles a wealthy silk merchant. He is nearly seven feet tall, terrifying to behold and he loves to eat.*

Setting:
Norfolk, England (sort of)
April 3, 1667 (more or less)

SOME THOUGHTS ABOUT THE PLAY

It is very long. Do it fast. This is a rough, aggressive age. It is very long. Do it fast, but make it real. It lives only if it addresses and presents relationships between real (and unreal) people with real, immense needs, and fears and hopes. Played rapidly without specificity and intelligence it will feel to the audience a million years long.

It is very long because it is full of words; it is, in fact, very much a play about words and writing. The words are not hurdles to leap across and over on your way to some big juicy inarticulate emotion, you American actors! The scenes full of words are not inaccurate and unreliable suggestions for some potential event to which the play alludes elliptically but does not actually describe, you American directors! The scenes must be read and analyzed carefully and precisely (specifically) and imaginatively (but groundedly) with an eye toward *objectives* and *needs* and *plausible psychological development*. The characters live and do what they come onstage to do (and they *always always* come onstage to *do* something) through their words.

Frequent address of the audience is fine; more than fine, it's important. The main relationships are between the characters but the audience ought to be included

Some Thoughts About the Play

when possible and not injurious to the life of the relationships onstage.

As for Dr Browne, his entire inner life, which is almost entirely articulated *(see play's Afterword)*, is shared directly with the audience. The audience, for him, *is* his inner life, or at least that to which his inner life is spoken.

The Set

Central should be Browne's deathbed, with a high marble headboard like a tombstone. The room should be richly appointed and cluttered with books, scrolls, astrolabes, telescopes, microscopes, models of engines, a model of the quarry, models of buildings, sacks of gold, musical instruments, anatomical charts, skulls of various animals including many human skulls, bottles of medicine, bottles with dead things and necrotic tissues floating inside, paintings (including several portraits of Browne), surveying equipment, nautical equipment, daggers and swords and harquebuses, abacuses—and a cobwebbed, long-unused writing desk with split pens, dried ink in dusty inkwells and great sheaves and stacks of paper, endlessly scribbled upon.

There is a plinth, empty, awaiting the arrival of the urn. When it arrives, the urn should be astonishing, blackened ancient terra-cotta with bas-relief faces in ghastly rictuses and agonies of death—coins on their eyes, tongues distended, jaws either rigor-mortised opened or clamped shut with mortuary bandage. It should be very sinister and old. It will be required to cough up a delicate spume of dust *and* belch forth a thick cloud of smoke. Smoke is smoke and dust is dust and a spume is different from a cloud and yes the urn must be able to do both of those things.

Music

His Soul's songs have been set to beautiful music by Mel Marvin (permission for use may be obtained through the Joyce Ketay Agency).

"There Is a Land of Pure Delight" is a traditional English hymn, and can be found in hymnals. The melody is traditional. The words are by Isaac Watts. It should be sung in four-part harmony.

Costumes

The costumes should be sumptuous and extravagant; neither leadenly historically accurate nor too silly! There should probably be a touch (only a touch) of the modern about the look of the characters, for instance, period clothing but no wigs. Remember that these people live in the country so wigs and other Restoration geegaws are probably not appropriate.

Browne's swollen body and Sarah's naked body in Scene Four should be achieved by anatomically articulated, over-the-top body stockings (genitals included). Real nudity is too...real.

The Accents

This is the way I described the accent issue in the first drafts:

> The aristocrats all speak standard American English, crisp and clear.
>
> The bumpkins speak a made-up dialect. Simply pronounce the words exactly as they are written—it will sound a little like Brooklynese, though it should not be done with a Brooklyn accent; its vocabulary is derived from Yorkshire, Brooklyn, and also *Krazy Kat* (the comic strip; not the cartoon). *It is not southern American, Texan, Irish or African-American!!* You will get it right if you just read it

Some Thoughts About the Play

out loud as it is spelled, *without accent of any kind.* They speak rapidly and clearly. To be understood by the audience you have to speak very very clearly. Schadenfreude's accent should be a great trilled and guttural German. (*Please,* actor playing Schadenfreude, do not substitute "sh" for "s"—be intelligible and crisp.) Estrelita's accent should be a great, rich, voluptuous Spanish. (Actor playing Estrelita, do *not* add an "e" to every word beginning with "s," and do not do a Castilian lisp.)

Dogwater's stutter, again, should be exactly as written—*please,* the actor playing him should *not* make up his own stutters, or add to the ones written. Dogwater has great control over his impediment and has the lightness and crispness that implies. Remember, he speaks for a living! Adding and improvising stuttering will kill the jokes and make the speeches interminable and unintelligible.

I would add to the above that it now seems to me *possible* that the whole thing could be done with British accents, the peasant dialect probably a Midlands dialect—though if this option is tried, the made-up peasant words wouldn't change, just the accent. I like the American sound but perhaps a British sound would work.

Because of the strangeness of the peasant language, regardless of which side of the Atlantic, accentually speaking, your production winds up on, you should play the first scenes with a special precision and care. Babbo and Maccabbee's first speeches will tend to affright audiences with their linguistic alienness, and must serve as an accessible, comprehensible template for listening to the play.

I hope Dogwater's stutter is not offensive to anyone with a stutter—several people with stutters have seen the play and have not taken offense, but using a disability in a comedy always raises complex questions. And Dogwater is a comic character—the audience should laugh at him, though not because he stutters. His stutter is another kind of eloquence, he is in magnificent control of it, unapologetic, though vulnerable, as we see at the end of Scene Two, to mockery. As I mentioned, this is a play about language and words, and I think the accents, made-up words, Dogwater's stutter and everyone's loquacity are all part of a general reveling in language and in the ways language is used.

Intermissions

There must be two intermissions, one after Act Two, one after Act Three. This means that the middle section is short; that's fine. Putting the second intermission after Act Four is a bad idea; having only one intermission is worse.

This play is dedicated
to the memory of
Dr Max Deutscher
1915–1980
scar-tough & skinless,
wrathful & wonderful…

Act One

CONTEMPTUS MUNDI

Bright Fresh Early April Morning

(The sickroom. The deathbed. Dr Browne lying in it, covered, rattling feebly, asleep. The curtains are drawn and it is dark. At the foot of the bed, on the floor, Maccabbee and Babbo are fucking.)

Maccabbee & Babbo: HUH HUH HUH HUH HUH HUH HUH!

Babbo: *(Sharply)* Sssshhh!

(They both sit up, look at the bed, see Dr Browne breathing, and go back to their copulation.)

Maccabbee & Babbo: HUH! HUH! HUH! HUH! HUH! HUH HUUUUUUUUUHHHH!!!!

(Babbo sticks her legs straight up in the air and her slippers fly over her head across the room. They have finished.)

Maccabbee: *(Fastening his pants)* Ouf.

Babbo: Shame.

Maccabbee: 'Tis natchural.

Babbo: Verra. But it still bin a shame. We shouldn't oughta a done dat. In here. Him dying onna bed 'n' you with da clap so bad yer nose is rot off.

MACCABBEE: Gets me going, da smella da room.

BABBO: Dat's disgusting.

MACCABBEE: I predick dat he takes his last breaf before noon. Ef he don't pop first. Dat's my scientific summestimation.

BABBO: Poor Dr Browne. So swole...

MACCABBEE: Think a all dem juices.

(They look at each other, a lascivious look.)

MACCABBEE: You wanna?

(As they begin to embrace again, DR BROWNE *sits up suddenly, makes an abrupt horrible noise, falls back and begins to spasm and gurgle.)*

BABBO: Ah Christ! We gone and disrespected him to da portals a death!

MACCABBEE: Go get da missus.

BABBO: *(Shrieking)* Aaaaahhh!!!

MACCABBEE: Da Event! 'Tis imminent! Scoot, 'n' hurry!

*(*BABBO *runs out one door,* MACCABBEE *the other. There is a simultaneous darkening and a build of strange, gray light. Music. Above the headboard a white ladder descends, just the tip, a light comes down from Heaven, and* HIS SOUL *strains upward, trying to reach the ladder; meanwhile* DEATH, *growling, enters the room and approaches the bed.* DEATH *lays a chilly hand on* DR BROWNE's *throat and from the sleeve of his cloak he draws a huge carving knife.)*

DEATH: At...last...I've...waited...so long...for you... THOMAS...come...I am ravenous...how I love—

*(*DEATH *raises the knife.)*

DR BROWNE: *(Sitting up, eyes still shut, fierce)* NOT YET, GODDAMNIT!

Act One

(The lights revert abruptly to normal, the music dies as though running out of batteries, DEATH growls in frustration and runs out the door; HIS SOUL gives up reaching for the ladder and drops down behind the headboard.)

HIS SOUL: Shit.

(The light from Heaven dies. DR BROWNE opens his eyes, shivers with cold, wide awake into terror.)

DR BROWNE: Maccabbee!

(MACCABBEE enters.)

MACCABBEE: Yup.

DR BROWNE: What's the date?

MACCABBEE: Thursday.

DR BROWNE: The *date*, you idiot.

MACCABBEE: April Three.

DR BROWNE: My Birthday.

MACCABBEE: No need ta call me a idiot.

DR BROWNE: *My Birthday.*

MACCABBEE: 'N' many happy returns a da day.

DR BROWNE: I will die today.

MACCABBEE: I said dat ta Babbo not five minutes gone. I predicket it. From da gurgle 'n' da gasp. 'Tis scientific.

DR BROWNE: I have trained you well. Fetch the gravedigger. It's morning?

MACCABBEE: Only just.

DR BROWNE: *(Lying back in bed)* Go.

(MACCABBEE runs out. HIS SOUL sticks its head up, rattles its chains.)

HIS SOUL: Soon! Soon!

DR BROWNE: Very soon.

HIS SOUL: You stink like a sewer! I can't bear this much longer.

DR BROWNE: *(Straining)* I can't release...it won't come out... *(He gives up.)*

*(*DAME DOROTHY BROWNE *hurries in.* HIS SOUL *disappears.)*

DAME DOROTHY: Are you...? Thank God.

DR BROWNE: Not yet. But soon...

*(*DAME DOROTHY *goes to windows, pulls open the big drapes. Morning light streams in.)*

DAME DOROTHY: Happy Birthday, Thomas. Did you pass a stool? *(Silence. She checks the bedpan. Empty)* Guess not.

DR BROWNE: I've swollen again.

DAME DOROTHY: You can't have swollen, you haven't eaten in a week.

*(*BABBO *rushes in.)*

BABBO: Bin dead?
(She sees him.)
Ahhh, thank God. Many happy returns, Dr Browne. You look spectacala.

DR BROWNE: I bloat.

BABBO: Mrs Browne, dose wimmin you let in last night, dey be making a harful warrick in da kitchen, be scarfin down da rah heggs 'n' sucking seeds outa da squash, 'n' one bin slavverin every dropta wine inna pantry. Fer breakfast.

DAME DOROTHY: I have to go now, Thomas. Thomas?

DR BROWNE: I want to see the gravedigger.

DAME DOROTHY: You don't need a gravedigger.

DR BROWNE: I have instructions—

Act One

BABBO: 'N' dey keept it up in halfta nour don't be nuffin potable ner comastible in da place, 'n' no food fer Dr Browne's funeral.

DAME DOROTHY: Babbo!

BABBO: 'N' you better come now 'cause I can't congle with 'em, 'n' twas your idea to let 'em in.

DR BROWNE: GRAVEDIGGER!

DAME DOROTHY: Babbo, stay here and watch till Dr Schadenfreude comes.

(She goes.)

DR BROWNE: I shouldn't scream. It brings on the bloating.

BABBO: Fer aftah da funeral, I thought maybe ta serve plum tart with lemmin grind. It's yer favorite. How'd dat be, Dr Browne?

DR BROWNE: I don't care…what you serve. I won't be there.

BABBO: Dat's true. But all same, 'tis yer funeral. 'N' you was always such a fussy 'n' patricula man.

DR BROWNE:
Last night
I dreamt I breathed
my final breath, and as I did
my soul
escaped,
rose out of me
like a fat, pale moon.
It floated to the ceiling.
It caught there
in the blackened roof beams,
and stuck. My dead eyes,
my dead eyes saw it wriggle like a fly,
trapped, not

able
to rise any higher.

(HIS SOUL *rattles its chains.*)

BABBO: *(Softly)* I think I'll make da tart. Dere bin early plums, so it be tarter dan usual, make everyone pucker 'n' deir eyes water like dey was crying fer you.

(She laughs a little.)

DR BROWNE: A good plan. There should be tears.

BABBO: I'll weep fer you, Sir Thomas.

DR BROWNE: Listen, old lady.

BABBO: Listet to what?

DR BROWNE: That pounding. In the distance. Rolling over the meadows. Boooomm. Boooommm. It's the sound of the engines in the quarry, digging deep.
My engines.
I don't want to die.

(MACCABBEE *and the gravedigger,* LEONARD PUMPKIN, *enter.*)

MACCABBEE: Da gravedigger.

(DR SCHADENFREUDE *enters.*)

MACCABBEE: 'N' da doctah.

DR BROWNE: It's my birthday.

DR SCHADENFREUDE: Congratulations. You look… appallingly bad. Your color— it's positively inorganic.

DR BROWNE: The leeches.

DR SCHADENFREUDE: In a minute. First—

DR BROWNE: What?

DR SCHADENFREUDE: A mercury enema!

DR BROWNE: *NO!*

Act One

(DR SCHADENFREUDE *pulls from his bag a frightful gadget, a large glass bottle filled with quicksilver, on one end a syringe plunger, on the other end large phallic-shaped leather nozzle.*)

DR SCHADENFREUDE: Yes.

DR BROWNE: I refuse.

DR SCHADENFREUDE: I'm your doctor.

DR BROWNE: I'll be dead soon. The leeches.

DR SCHADENFREUDE: Patience. First the enema. We have to try to remove that blockage. Ladies leave.

(BABBO *goes.* DR SCHADENFREUDE *notices the gravedigger.*)

DR SCHADENFREUDE: Who are you?

PUMPKIN: Gravedigger.

DR SCHADENFREUDE: How convenient. Now then.

(DR SCHADENFREUDE *leaps onto the bed with the equipment. He pulls the sheets over his head, which mercifully obscures from our sight the procedure. There is much struggling.*)

MACCABBEE: *(To* PUMPKIN*)* He's gotta tumor. Inna bowels. Like a onion, dey say. Plug him up.

PUMPKIN: A onion?

MACCABBEE: Inna bowels.

PUMPKIN: Gawd.

(DR SCHADENFREUDE *is finished.*)

DR SCHADENFREUDE: No good. Gunpowder couldn't budge it. Let's bleed him a little.

DR BROWNE: *(Weakly)* Leeches...

DR SCHADENFREUDE: Yes, but first we skim off the bad blood, so the leeches don't get sick when they suck. You're a regular sack of toxins, Thomas.

(DR SCHADENFREUDE *takes out a horrible-looking device, like a sap-spigot for syrup gathering; he rams it in* DR BROWNE'S *side, and holds a bucket underneath it to catch the blood, which is running out at an alarming rate.*)

DR BROWNE: I'm…so…cold…no…more…

(The lights change. Music. HIS SOUL *sits up, looking eager.* DR SCHADENFREUDE, MACCABBEE *and* PUMPKIN *can't see this.* DR SCHADENFREUDE *pulls out the spigot, applies a wad of cotton to the puncture.)*

DR SCHADENFREUDE: Enough for now.

(The lights go back to normal.)

HIS SOUL: *(Disappearing)* DAMN!

DR SCHADENFREUDE: And already your color's improving! The wonders of the modern age. Fifty years ago these techniques were unknown. And now the leeches!
Thomas?
Sir Thomas?

(DR BROWNE *is unconscious.* DR SCHADENFREUDE *slaps him gently.)*

DR SCHADENFREUDE: Peacefully resting. No leeches for today… Well maybe just one.
(He applies a disgusting leech.)
Smack smack smack. Little crescent kisses.

(DR SCHADENFREUDE *to* PUMPKIN, *who has moved away:)*

DR SCHADENFREUDE: Squeamish?

PUMPKIN: Nope.

DR SCHADENFREUDE: Hard to be squeamish and work in your field. Why don't I know you?

PUMPKIN: New to these parts.

DR SCHADENFREUDE: Name?

Act One

PUMPKIN: Pumpkin.

DR SCHADENFREUDE: Christian name?

PUMPKIN: Leonard.

DR SCHADENFREUDE: What happened to the old gravedigger?

PUMPKIN: Died.

DR SCHADENFREUDE: Your predecessor and I had an agreement. I pay crown sterling for reasonably intact cadavers. Dr Schadenfreude.

(He proffers his hand. PUMPKIN *shakes it.* DR SCHADENFREUDE *wipes it with a hankie.)*

DR SCHADENFREUDE: Medical research. Highly scientific work. Right, Maccabbee?

MACCABBEE: Oh, yoop.

DR SCHADENFREUDE: How are Browne's experiments coming along?

MACCABBEE: Well, Doctah Browne mostly loss interest inna lass few weeks, oncet da swelling incepted. We was doing a experiment ta see if da dogs would eat rotted birds.

DR SCHADENFREUDE: Did they?

MACCABBEE: O sure dey bin chompet on stuff so rotted da flies wouldn't go near it.

DR SCHADENFREUDE: From which you conclude…

MACCABBEE: Da conclusions was fer Sir Thomas ta extrapolate 'n' send to da Royal Academy in London. I mostly took care a da nasty stuff. But I guess…I conclude…dat dogs…like rotted meat.

DR SCHADENFREUDE: And *thrive* from eating it.

MACCABBEE: Yah, dey do at dat. 'Tis nauseating.

DR SCHADENFREUDE: From which we may conclude, perhaps, that there is a vitality in putrefaction, a life in death: rats born in sacks of mouldy grain, maggots blossoming in rancid meat, bustle bugs in the water-tap scumbeard—

MACCABBEE: Science bin amazement!

DR SCHADENFREUDE: Browne's last Will and Testament. Is it available for viewing?

MACCABBEE: Han't heard nuffin about it.

DR SCHADENFREUDE: *(Flipping* MACCABBEE *a coin)* If you happen to hear that he's specified the name of his eulogist, fill me in. I'm certain I'll be asked to eulogize him. I knew him inside and out! Everyone says he was a genius. They say the king himself might attend... *(To* PUMPKIN*)* Mendicants, vagrants, charity corpses—as long as they're reasonably fresh.

(DR SCHADENFREUDE *starts out as* DAME DOROTHY *enters.)*

DR SCHADENFREUDE: *(Bowing)* Dame Dorothy.

DAME DOROTHY: It's his birthday. He says he'll die today.

DR SCHADENFREUDE: Cradle to crypt, a mark of character. The Romans did it.

DAME DOROTHY: By killing themselves.

DR SCHADENFREUDE: Better a warm bath and a sharp knife than a slow, wasting death. Your husband I'm sure would agree with me. If he was conscious. Madame. *(Bows and goes)*

DAME DOROTHY: Maccabbee, show him out.

MACCABBEE: *(Gesturing for* PUMPKIN *to leave)* Dis way, Pumpkin.

Act One 11

DAME DOROTHY: No, not him. He can stay for a moment. Show the doctor out.

MACCABBEE: Da doctah's been here every day fer a month. He knows how ta get out.

DAME DOROTHY: Well, just in case.

MACCABBEE: In case what?

DAME DOROTHY: Maccabbee, go!

MACCABBEE: *(Pointing to* PUMPKIN*)* How come he getsa stay?

DAME DOROTHY: I want to discuss the sarcophagus.

MACCABBEE: Da what?

(DAME DOROTHY *points to the door and glowers.* MACCABBEE *grudgingly exits.*)

DAME DOROTHY: Leonard.

PUMPKIN: Dorfy.

DAME DOROTHY: Wait.

(DAME DOROTHY *tiptoes to* DR BROWNE, *assures herself that he is unconscious, checks the door and windows, then goes to* PUMPKIN *and kisses him passionately.*)

PUMPKIN: *(Pulling away)* DORFY!

DAME DOROTHY: He's sleeping.

PUMPKIN: 'Tis perverse.

DAME DOROTHY: I know. I haven't seen you since Monday evening.

PUMPKIN: Busy week. Dropping like—

DAME DOROTHY: *(Throatily)* Come here. Leonard…

PUMPKIN: I mean, look at him. Poor ole balloon.

DAME DOROTHY: I don't want to look at him.

PUMPKIN: Let's go to da woods.

DAME DOROTHY: *(Pulling him down to the rug)* I can't leave. My place is here, with my husband.

PUMPKIN: Ent you sad he bin dying?

DAME DOROTHY: Grief...is a highly personal thing. It's spring, Leonard. I've been cold a long time. Your hands are so strong and so filthy.

PUMPKIN: Grave dirt.

DAME DOROTHY: Poor Pumpkin, you work so hard.

PUMPKIN: My poor back be stabbat harful bya enna da day.

DAME DOROTHY: Because to bury the dead you must dig deep.

PUMPKIN: Head-high from da bottom a da hole.

DAME DOROTHY: Poor Thomas, in the ground. After he's gone, we'll dig nothing deeper than the two-foot pit a seed-potato needs. Little rows of vegetables, on our small and fertile farm.

PUMPKIN: Fuck be dat. Bin a gentleman farmer den, own da biggest farm fer miles, hire some poor lob ta plant da vegetals fer me. 'N' da machines ta dig limestone from da quarry.

(Silence. DAME DOROTHY looks away.)

DAME DOROTHY: I hate the quarry.

PUMPKIN: You make a swollot a money outa dat quarry.

DAME DOROTHY: Nothing good will come from it.

PUMPKIN: Limestone come from it.

DAME DOROTHY: Those women in the kitchen. Did you see them?

PUMPKIN: Ah, nope.

DAME DOROTHY: Three ranter women.

PUMPKIN: Ranters bin heretics.

DAME DOROTHY: They used to live in cottages on a farm—on the land Thomas's father bought, where Thomas dug the quarry. They had a little farm there.

PUMPKIN: Stupid a dem to do dat, set a farm on dat rocky soil. You shouldn'ta oughta take dem in, dey han't gonna wanna leave. 'N' steal yer eyes out yer sockets. 'N' got contagious lice.

DAME DOROTHY: I have a dream almost every night. Thomas has died and his soul gone off to the judgment seat. And been damned, poor Thomas. He looks for hell, but he can't find the entrance. Then he does find it, and it's at the bottommost pit in the quarry. There's a sinkhole, like a drain, small, and he slips down it and disappears. And sometimes the dream doesn't end there. Sometimes I'm being pulled in after him.

PUMPKIN: 'Tis silly.

DAME DOROTHY: Their cottages were burnt when the land was seized. They sleep in ditches.
None of the children will come home to see him die.

(From offstage there is a voice calling:)

DR DOGWATER: D-d-Dame D-Dorothy! Duh-duh-duh-Dame Duh-Dorothy!

PUMPKIN: Shit beans, it's da pastor!

(They scramble to respectable dress and distance as DR DOGWATER bursts in.)

DR DOGWATER: Good morning, Dame Dorothy. How's the puh-patient? Improving?

DAME DOROTHY: Quite the opposite.

DR DOGWATER: Optimism, optimism—he's resting puh-puh-peacefully.

DAME DOROTHY: He's nearly dead.

DR DOGWATER: Ah. Tuh-too bad. I hope he's resigned. Have you had a chuh-chance to look over those papers I left?

DAME DOROTHY: I've been preoccupied.

DR DOGWATER: Yes, this is a tuh-trying time for you, I understand, but buh-business affairs press on, and not even the guh-grim reaper can hold them in abeyance. I suh-speak now, of course, not as your suh-spiritual adviser but as your fuh-future partner in commerce. The quarry expansion depends on your cuh-cooperation.

PUMPKIN: You bin expandet da quarry?

DR DOGWATER: Huh-who are you?

PUMPKIN: Da new gravedigger, namet Pumpkin.

DR DOGWATER: Aha. And you're interested in quarrying, Mr. Pumpkin?

PUMPKIN: Ah, yup. I bin verra interested in da development a industry.

DR DOGWATER: Splendid! And so you shuh-should be! A tuh-true man of the age! You're a Protestant, of course.

PUMPKIN: Yessir, I always bin dat.

DR DOGWATER: You see before you, Dame Duh-Dorothy, luh-living proof of my contention: that the vuh-violent and irruptive nah-nah-nature of these times is no cause for despair. Leave despair to the weak and the gah-gaseous, to the Catholics. You were born poor?

PUMPKIN: In da verra bogs a deprivation.

DR DOGWATER: And now you're a puh-puh-prospering gravedigger!

PUMPKIN: I han't exactly prospering but—

Act One

DR DOGWATER: But you'll keep duh-digging till you reach your puh-pot of gold, right?
How rich do you thuh-think Sir Thomas Browne was, Puh-Pumpkin? Very rich?

PUMPKIN: Ah, yup.

DR DOGWATER: Enormously rich?

DAME DOROTHY: Dr Dogwater, this is hardly an appropriate time to be counting my husband's money.

DR DOGWATER: It's instructive, Muh-Mrs Browne. Pumpkin, this man was—uh, *is* extremely wealthy. You could bury the entire parish and nuh-not earn half of what he makes in one day just luh-lying here and letting his puh-puh-profits accumulate. He's puh-practically muh-made of gold. Do you want to be rich like that, Pumpkin?

PUMPKIN: I haspire to dat, pastor, ef I work fer it—

DR DOGWATER: Once we thought Heaven glowed with the light of divine fire, Dame Dorothy, but now we *know*—it glows with the shine of gold. In the fuh-firmament, a suh-sun of gold that makes men like this man tuh-twitch, and writhe, and work. You wuh-worry about expanding the quarry and dislocating squatters, but here is my argument made flesh—this man. Scrape the lichen from the rock, expose it to the rays of that muh-muh-metal sun, give it guh-gainful employment, and watch it grow into something more nuh-noble than suh-suh-scum.

PUMPKIN: So you gonna expandet da quarry?

DR DOGWATER: I am not accustomed to discussing my business with hired help. Good day.

(Pause)

PUMPKIN: I bin going. Pastor. I appreciatet da instructet. Missus.

(He goes.)

DAME DOROTHY: There was no cause for impoliteness, Dr Dogwater, you shouldn't have spoken so abruptly.

DR DOGWATER: You have a suh-soft heart, Dame Dorothy, and that befits a wuh-woman, but after Sir Thomas is d...is d...d...d...

DAME DOROTHY: Dead.

DR DOGWATER: ...and keeping the cuh-company of angels in puh-paradise you will be chuh-chief shareholder in the Nuh-nuh-Norfolk and London Limestone Quarrying Company. And you will need a sterner, more ruh-rigorous mien. Your huh-husband lacked that. He hoarded gold, too timid in the muh-marketplace.

DAME DOROTHY: He was fearful of loss.

DR DOGWATER: Wuh-well put. But God hates idle money as much as he hates idle men. Suh-Sir Thomas could not be muh-moved to reinvest in the buh-business. We hope his widow will—

DAME DOROTHY: Could we discuss this another time.

DR DOGWATER: Of course. Thoughtless of me. After the fuh-funeral. Tomorrow, perhaps.

DAME DOROTHY: And we really don't know if the shares have been left to me, or if they've been left to anyone at all. If there's no Will—

DR DOGWATER: If there's no wuh-wuh...OF COURSE THERE'S A WUH-WILL. Uh isn't there?

DAME DOROTHY: I have no idea. He loves making messes, leaving them behind.

DR DOGWATER: Muh-much more than a muh-mess! The Buh-Book of the Apocalypse couldn't compare. The cuh-crown will confiscate the entire estate, the cuh-quarry would become cuh-crown lands, the

Act One

kuh-king, long may he reign, is a vuh-veritable muh-muh-Mammon, ah-ah-avaricious! He's appropriating absolutely everything he can get his guh-greedy ruh-royal mitts on, we'll all be ah-utterly utterly utterly destroyed if Browne dies without a Will! Puh-Panic! Puh-Panic! He'll have to tell us where it is, or write a new one.

DAME DOROTHY: He won't write anything anymore. He says the smell of ink makes him nauseous.

DR DOGWATER: But Dame Dorothy he's a writer.

DAME DOROTHY: Apparently no longer.

DR DOGWATER: Duh-Dame Dorothy, this is no joke. We have to get him to tell us where he put the document *(Screaming very loudly)* WHEN HE WAKES UP!

(DR BROWNE *wakes with a start.*)

DAME DOROTHY: Doctor Dogwater!

DR BROWNE: Am I dead?

DAME DOROTHY: No, Thomas.

HIS SOUL: *(Appearing)* NO! NO! NO! *(It disappears again)*

DR BROWNE: There are moles tunneling underneath this house. I can hear them, burrowing. They are undermining the foundation. Fetch the mole dogs. Where's the gravedigger? He was here. Has the urn arrived?

DAME DOROTHY: Not yet.

DR DOGWATER: Uh-urn?

DR BROWNE: Excavated. In the digging. Right there in the quarry, a mound of some sort. An urn in the heart of it. Containing hair, teeth and bones. No idea whose remains. Saxon, maybe. Roman, perhaps. Perhaps earlier even than that…

(To Dr Dogwater*)* Who are you? Dorothy, who is this man?

DAME DOROTHY: It's Dr Dogwater, Thomas, you know Dr Dogw—

DR BROWNE: A doctor? Can he do something about the moles? Is this your leech?

*(*Dr Browne *plucks* Dr Schadenfreude's *leech, now swollen, from beneath his nightshirt and tosses it to* Dr Dogwater, *who catches it, then realizes what he's holding.)*

DR DOGWATER: Luh-luh-luh-LEEEECH!

*(*Dr Dogwater *flings the leech into the audience.)*

DAME DOROTHY: Thomas, it's Dr Dogwater, your pastor, your old, old friend.

DR DOGWATER: And buh-business puh-puh-partner. L-Leviticus Dogwater.

*(*Dr Browne *glares at* Dr Dogwater *without recognition.)*

DR BROWNE: I never saw you before.

DAME DOROTHY: Thomas!

DR DOGWATER: Oh, d-dear, he's l-lost his wuh-wits.

DR BROWNE: I studied embryology with Fabricius in Padua, Doctor whoever-you-are; the great Fabricius, did you know that? The chick in the egg. The baby in the...the genesis of things.
I was a physician but I stuck to research. I couldn't cure people. Christ did that, or so they say. Well, I'm sure he did. I couldn't. I wrote things...
My experiments led me from embryology to engineering to excavation to urns and my current fascination with burial...customs.
(Little pause)
Unearth the urn,

pop it open
with a pick,
remove the skull:
crack it, brown,
like a nut, and
in the bowl, in the
seat
of the soul…
not even dust.
Just the tattered white filaments
of some spidery event.
(*Little pause*)
It is impossible
to conclude
anything.
I know who you are, Dogwater.

DR DOGWATER: Hah-how are you today, Sir Thomas?

DR BROWNE: Mortal.

DR DOGWATER: Muh-muh-muh—

DR BROWNE: And fading. I cannot shit. All plugged up; no place to go.

DR DOGWATER: I will puh-pray for you.

DR BROWNE: I'd sell my soul for a bowel movement.

HIS SOUL: You would! I know you would! You never valued me!

DR DOGWATER: Tuh-Thomas, we were just tah-talking and wuh-wondering if your wuh-Will had buh-been completed.

DR BROWNE: My Will.

DR DOGWATER: Y-yes. Nuh-now is the time to be letting guh-go of worldly things, tuh-turning your thoughts to suh-salvation and the uh-unimaginable delights of puh-puh-puh-paradise.

(HIS SOUL *rattles its chains wistfully.*)

DR BROWNE: Paradise.

HIS SOUL: Paradise! You keep me from paradise, you swollen stinkbag, wormfood—die!
(It goes away.)

DR BROWNE: You want to know if I've made a Will.

DR DOGWATER: Yes.

DR BROWNE: Did I, Dorothy?

DAME DOROTHY: I think so, yes.

DR BROWNE: *(To* DR DOGWATER*)* Yes.

DR DOGWATER: Guh-good. Nuh-now I—

DR BROWNE: You want to know where the Will is.

DR DOGWATER: Wuh-well, I—

DR BROWNE: I have no idea.

DR DOGWATER: Tuh-Thomas, this is nah-nah-not a juh-joking mah-mah-mah—

DR BROWNE: When I was a medical student in Padua, I often visited the Jewish Ghetto there. Because I wanted to know if it was true.

(Small pause)

DR DOGWATER: Wha… What's true?

DR BROWNE: If it was true what they say about old Jews dying. Do you know what they say about old Jews dying?

DR DOGWATER: Nah-nah—

DR BROWNE: Dorothy, do you know?

DAME DOROTHY: Where's the Will, Thomas? Dr Dogwater wants to see it.

Act One

DR BROWNE: They say when an old Jew is about to die, and he wants to be left...*alone*...with his Deity, he turns his face to the wall.

(DR BROWNE *does this. There is silence.*)

DR BROWNE: The other Jews understand this to be a sign that they should absent themselves.

DAME DOROTHY: Thomas—

DR BROWNE: And they *do*. They *leave*.

(DAME DOROTHY *and* DR DOGWATER *look at each other.*)

DAME DOROTHY: Perhaps we should leave.

DR DOGWATER: But he isn't Jewish.

(BABBO *bursts in, carrying an unbaked tart.*)

BABBO: Secuse me again, Mrs Browne, but dem three knacky women in da kitchen bin movet to da pantry now 'n' be coombin over da silver 'n' one stufftet halfta da tea service in her pockets.

DR DOGWATER: Thieves!

DAME DOROTHY: Not thieves, just three harmless ranter women...

DR DOGWATER: Ruh-ranters!? What are ruh-ranters doing in your house?

BABBO: Well right now dey bin stealet evahthing dat han't bin screwed down 'r locked up.

DAME DOROTHY: They were hungry, it was cold last night, I...

DR DOGWATER: A sterner mien, Mrs Browne! Ruh-ranters are debauched heretics. Cuh-come. We'll see to this puh-pillaging together. Buh-buh-Browne, your house is in duh-duh-disarray. Remember, God expects Man to d...to d...to d...

DR BROWNE: To die.

DR DOGWATER: Just so. In a responsible and ah-orderly fah-fah-fashion.

(DR DOGWATER *and* DAME DOROTHY *go.* BABBO *starts to follow them.*)

DR BROWNE: Halt, imponderably old and faithful retainer.

BABBO: Me?

DR BROWNE: *(Searching under the mattress)* Who else? I want you to hide something.

(He produces the Will, a slender document wax-sealed, lawyer-stamped, wrapped in black ribbon and bordered in black.)

BABBO: Bin you writet another book?

DR BROWNE: God forbid.

BABBO: Hamen ta dat.

DR BROWNE: My Will. Everyone's clamoring for a copy, it's the most popular thing I ever wrote. Hide it, Babbo, I'll let you know when it's wanted. Hide it well.

(BABBO *crams the Will inside the tart.*)

DR BROWNE: Oh. Well...um, alright, you... You'll, uh... remember to take it out before you bake it.

BABBO: A course, Doctah, I bin old but my memory bin sharp as a... Sharp as a... Uh...

DR BROWNE: Tack?

BABBO: Right! So han't be worret, Doctah Greene.

DR BROWNE: Browne.

BABBO: Da tarts come out nicet. Gotta go get da chickens ready fer broasting.

(She goes.)

*(*HIS SOUL *sits up.)*

Act One

HIS SOUL: Can't you release me? Can't you let me go? You see how I suffer.

DR BROWNE: *(Trying)* I can't...unclench.

HIS SOUL: You hoard everything. It's only justice that you should die of constipation.

DR BROWNE: Don't hate me so terribly.

HIS SOUL: I want a divorce.

DR BROWNE: I fed you well. I read Latin and Greek, philosophy and mathematics, all for you. All food for you.

HIS SOUL: You tried. It never worked. Everything had to pass through you. All that meat. We must divide possessions now, and part company.

DR BROWNE: I picked wildflowers, I gawped at the moon, I prayed devotedly to God for your redemption—

HIS SOUL: Redeem me then. DIE! I want nothing weighty, no ballast when I ascend. Nothing you've touched and polluted. The house, the gold, the quarry, all yours. I only want a small shard of an idea.

DR BROWNE: I thought...I thought I'd *want* to die today but I'm so...afraid. Don't leave me.

HIS SOUL: You used to be able to close your eyes and see the light of Heaven.

DR BROWNE: That was very long ago.

HIS SOUL: I know. Now when you close your eyes...

DR BROWNE: A kind of dull brown and red darkness.

HIS SOUL: Mostly that, yes, but—

DR BROWNE: Daylight diffused through flesh. Nothing else.

HIS SOUL: Liar! There's one small speck of fire in there, one pure dot of light flickering, imperiled, but there!

DR BROWNE: Paradise.

HIS SOUL: You try to hide it from me!

DR BROWNE: Reduced to that pinprick.

HIS SOUL: But paradise even so! Mine!

DR BROWNE: I'll have to think about it.

HIS SOUL: Don't think! Don't do that! Just give! If you think you'll extinguish it! Relinquish it to me!

DR BROWNE: Paradise. *(He's beginning to nod out.)* What do I think of Paradise? Listen. The machines. Boooomm. Booooom...Parad...
(He's asleep.)

HIS SOUL: Miser! After all I've done for you! You have to examine even that, that one atomie of gold; never valued it before, but now that I want it, you can't resist fingering it till it's tarnished, cheap brass like all the other goods in your cobwebbed musty little brass shop. Brazen hoarder. I hope you burst.

(As HIS SOUL *is railing the ranter women have snuck in and gathered round the bed.)*

SARAH: *(Looking at* HIS SOUL*)* Bin talket to his soul.

(HIS SOUL *sinks from view.)*

MARY: What it say?

RUTH: Say liberty. Say justice fer all da fellow creatures, Mary. Say peace 'n' food 'n' land, 'n' whilst it weepet fer da homeless 'n' afflictet dis windgall here get bored 'n' fall asleep.

SARAH: Muttering paradise.

RUTH: Be a good time ta rant, 'n' set up a hoo-hah dat shake da thatch from da roof 'n' buggle da peeps from out his yead. 'N' do it now. Da louse be dead before

Act One

you knowit. 'N' dat pastor almost took us pinching da silver.

SARAH: I got a lovely big spoon. Verra pretty spoon.

RUTH: *(Beginning to rant)* By da verra balls a da bleedet Christ, by da withered dugs a Mary, by da stripet socks a Joseph...

(All three start to shake in the grip of something powerful. MARY *snaps out of it and stops* RUTH.*)*

MARY: Hold it, Ruth, fer Christ sake, caused oncet you get ranting all three of us commencet. 'N' Sarah ent said ready. 'N' 'tis fer da memory a her poor mama we come here.

*(*DR BROWNE *stirs.)*

SARAH: Da puffball squirmet, be waket soon. Him dreamet some foul, sweaty dream, some guilty racket him. Soon we rant, not yet. I gotta feel da time.

RUTH: *(Hissing in* DR BROWNE's *ear)* Earfen clot.

MARY: Hist Ruth, 'n' come away.

(They exit.)

DR BROWNE: *(Waking slowly)* There's a ship on a dark river, fed by frozen streams, feeding an arctic ocean; my coffin ship. It's creaking.
(He calls to HIS SOUL*)* Are you there? Can we... negotiate?
Leave me then. Losing you is less than losing nothing, you incorporeal nonentity.
Maccabbee! MACCABBEE!
I mustn't shout, it—

*(*MACCABBEE *enters.)*

MACCABBEE: Whatchoo want?

DR BROWNE: A final experiment. Fetch three live chickens and—

MACCABBEE: You oughta rest, converse yer strength, Dr Browne, keep da experiments fer later—

DR BROWNE: My later is gone. I have to know… something. Fetch three live chickens.

MACCABBEE: Three live chickens.

DR BROWNE: Weigh each one.

MACCABBEE: Weigh each one.

DR BROWNE: Then strangle them.

MACCABBEE: A course.

DR BROWNE: Wait a few minutes after they die, and then weigh them again. Bring me the results.

MACCABBEE: Da strangled chickens?

DR BROWNE: No, *cretin*. The weights. Pre- and postmortem weights.

MACCABBEE: No need ta call names.

DR BROWNE: Chicken A weighs…six pounds. Alive. Does it weigh less when it's dead?
If it does, then something…has been lost.
If it weighs the same dead as alive then it has lost… nothing at all. Nothing of substance.

MACCABBEE: What could it lose?

DR BROWNE: It could lose…its soul.

MACCABBEE: Awww, Dr Browne, dat's nuts. Chickens han't got souls.

DR BROWNE: It has some vital spirit, some ether that impells its heart to beat, some shock or force; call it what you will, but there's nothing living without that… And I must know its weight, the awful weight of the soul, before…

MACCABBEE: Before what, Dr Browne?

DR BROWNE: Nothing. You're right. It is…nuts. I…

Why is there no one here to comfort me?
I'm swelling. Leave me. But...Maccabbee.

MACCABBEE: What, Dr Browne?

DR BROWNE: Keep your eyes on the ground. Watch for little holes.

MACCABBEE: ???

DR BROWNE: Mole holes. Tunnel mouths. A mixture of cyanide and boiling lye...
Get out of here.
The chicken experiment. Do it. I'm...already underway, and I have to know...
The ropes on the dock are slipping from the moorings, and I'm ...off...

(He's off, unconscious.)

MACCABBEE: Fetch da rottet birds, pickle dis gamey fish, count da ribs a dat poison snake, strangle three chickens. Maybe when he's dead I'll go help da German cut up his cadavers. Science bin slavery. 'N' ent one a dem knows how ta cure my clap.

(DR BROWNE *begins to rattle.*)

MACCABBEE: Doctah?

(Rattle)

MACCABBEE: Doctah?

(A really alarming gasp, then a huge expulsion of breath, and the lights begin to change slowly and the death music is heard.)

MACCABBEE: Dat soundet like da terminal hexpiration ta me. Before noon, like I prognosticated. Funny dere were no last words, he was always so talkative.

(DEATH *enters, growling, with his carving knife at the ready.* HIS SOUL *sits up as the ladder to heaven appears.*)

(MACCABBEE *senses something creepy afoot and slinks out, frightened.*)

(DEATH *approaches the bed and* HIS SOUL *reaches up toward the ladder.*)

(*A hooded figure*—THE ABBESS OF X—*enters stealthily.*)

HIS SOUL: I begin to climb; I have far to go; with every rung the weight of your contamination will fall from me, like a moulting bird I lessen and lighten and loose these chains...

DEATH: Thomas...my child, the bitter hour, the wasting hour has come. I come for you, I ache for you, lamentable, lamentable, I...your flesh, sweet heart, to rend at last...

THE ABBESS OF X: (*She is aware of neither* DEATH *nor His Soul*) Thomas?

HIS SOUL: To Paradise!

THE ABBESS OF X: THOMAS!

DEATH: Mine, flower, mine...

THE ABBESS OF X: God in Heaven, I've come too late.

(*She takes out a breviary, a rosary, a vial of holy water, and begins to murmur the Extreme Unction, in Latin.*)

DR BROWNE: Father...

DEATH: (*Raising his knife*) Thomas...

DR BROWNE: Father...

HIS SOUL: Good-bye!

DR BROWNE: Fa...ther...in to your hands...

HIS SOUL: Say it!

DR BROWNE: Into your hands I...

THE ABBESS OF X: Thomas. Thomas, can you hear me? Where's the Will, Thomas? Who did you name in The Will!?

Act One 29

HIS SOUL: *(Prompting)* COMMEND…MY…

DR BROWNE: MY…I COMMEND MY… *(Hearing what* HIS SOUL *is prompting him toward)* NO! I…*CONDEMN* MY…SPIR—

HIS SOUL: NO!

DR BROWNE: *(Forcing himself awake)* NO!

(DR BROWNE *sits up violently. He sees* THE ABBESS OF X—HE SCREAMS! *He turns to see* DEATH *with his raised knife*—HE REALLY SCREAMS! DEATH *screams and with a growl runs away. The music scratches off with the sound of a needle swept off a phonograph record. The lights bump back and* THE ABBESS OF X *rolls under the bed seconds before* DAME DOROTHY, DR DOGWATER *and* BABBO *run in.* HIS SOUL *is stunned at the sudden reversal.)*

HIS SOUL: HOW!? HOW!? YOU WERE DEAD, YOU HAD DIED, YOU'D TURNED TO CLAY, WHAT RESUSCITATED YOU?

(HIS SOUL *slips behind the bed. The ladder disappears.*)

DAME DOROTHY: Thomas, can you hear me? Are you alright?

DR BROWNE: I…am…not…sure…

BABBO: Praise be, praise be, bin snatchet from da grinning yawp a doom!

DR BROWNE: My sister was here.

DAME DOROTHY: No, Thomas, your sister is dead.

DR BROWNE: But she was here. She spoke Latin and sprinkled water, and look, the pillow is wet.

DR DOGWATER: Tuh-Thomas, y-your suh-sister d-d… perished in a shuh-shuh-shuh-shuh-shipwreck. Y-years ago. Duh-drowned.

DR BROWNE: But she was here. Resurrected. With… him.

DAME DOROTHY: There's no one here, Thomas.

DR BROWNE: And he's been dead longer than she. He had the knife, I remember that knife. Old monster.

DAME DOROTHY: Dr Dogwater, what's he talking about?

DR DOGWATER: Bah-bah-bah...I duh-duh-don't...

DR BROWNE: *(After a little pause, listening, then)* Another ship...from warmer seas...is sailing here...for me.
And listen, the machines. Hard at work. Moving earth. Boooom. Boooom. Boooom. Boooom.
To beat
the little
gentle man
who comes
to undo.
(He's out.)

DR DOGWATER: I-is he...?

(DR DOGWATER *tiptoes up to* DR BROWNE, *and gently pinches* DR BROWNE's *nostrils shut;* DR BROWNE *starts snoring through his mouth.*)

DAME DOROTHY: The engines give me nightmares and headaches. But they tranquilize him.

DR DOGWATER: Wuh-once, he b-bade me listen to the sound. The puh-pounding sound they make. Buh-boom. Buh-booom. Luh-listen, Dogwater, he s-said. Guh-God's timpani. Buh-booom.
I thought I'd use that ah-anecdote in the eu-eu-eulogy. Buh-booom.
Cuh-call me if he wuh-wakes. Wh-when he does. We've guh-got to find out about that wuh-wuh-wuh-Will.

(DR DOGWATER *leaves.* BABBO *and* DAME DOROTHY *sit, watching* DR BROWNE *sleep.*)

Act One

(The three ranter women enter, sit quietly around the bed. They look at DAME DOROTHY *and she looks at them, and everyone looks at the dying man.)*

*(*HIS SOUL *sits up and begins to sing softly.)*

HIS SOUL: *(Singing:)*

There is a little house in Heaven
Built of brick and wood,
In a shady and restricted
Crime-free neighborhood.
The shutters and the doors are painted
Bright cerulean blue;
And vines of morning glories climb,
Bloom-eternal in their prime,
Free of gravity and time,
Purple-white and fresh with dew,
Flower-mouth of Very-God
The Day does not divide in two.

And here in Heaven
I will never die.
I can say that
And not feel
I'm telling
A lie.
In Heaven I will never die.
Never
Never
Never
Die.

Act Two

IN WHAT TORNE SHIP SOEVER I EMBARKE

The Hard Light of Later Morning, the Glare of Noon

(DAME DOROTHY, *the three ranter women, and* BABBO *watch* DR BROWNE, *who is asleep.*)

MARY: *(With glowing gentleness)* Da kingdom a God be da kingdom a da earf. Dere bin no Heaven and no Hell, but only dis: da doings a da fellow creatures as dey dwell in dis world. Dat's what da ranters say. When Christ come again he come inta da flesh a wimmin 'n' da flesh a men, 'n' den all dat walk be good 'n' golden creatures 'n' kind. Dat's what da ranters say.

RUTH: Quarry land bin common land fer alla way back to da Garden a Heden, 'n' I care not a pin ner a fart fer his paper a ownership. What own? My little cottage burnet. My shitten rocky farm dug up. Now dey say, ef you wanna eat go work fer da swollen stench Browne and his devil digs. Fuck be dat.

SARAH: My ma bin a witch, Dame Dorothy, a forest witch. Han't been much good at it; mostly deliver babbies with a coupla harmless tricks. Dat's all. A good fellow creature 'n' ranter; she teachet me, 'n' we livet inna woods by Bury St Edmunds till dey encloset da woods, 'n' den da trouble come.

DAME DOROTHY: Bury St Edmunds.

SARAH: You know dat name. My ma curset da squire dat bought da woods, 'n' even though she han't got no talent 'n' her curses nevah carry, da squire go white 'n' freaket, 'n' his yeart stop beatet, 'n' he die, 'n' dey arrest my ma 'n' dis other woman fer witchcraft. 'N' dat other woman bin lessa a witch den my ma, she han't even call herself a witch, bin just a woman.

DAME DOROTHY: Your mother was—

SARAH: *(Nodding)* 'N' no one think more'n a flogging's likely, since dey han't hung a witch fer forty year, but den dey call fer a witness inna trial; a great thinker 'n' man a words, a doctor.

DAME DOROTHY: Oh God.

SARAH: Just bin knightet by da king. Bin a sir.

(Silence. They all look at DR BROWNE.*)*

SARAH: 'N' he talket, talket like a angel sing, but his words bin wicked, twisty words, 'n' bya time he shut his yatch dey got my ma swinget by a rough old rope. 'N' dat bin da enna my mama on dis earf.

DAME DOROTHY: Please. He was used. He never intended that. He thought he was raising a few harmless points, minor theological speculation. He came home with a fever, he didn't sleep for weeks.

SARAH: Dat happent ten year ago. 'N' last week we bin headet fer da wilds a Scotland; my ma come ta me 'n' say: "Sarah, turn about 'n' vistet him on his deathbed. Bring him a blessting from me."

DAME DOROTHY: But your mother—

SARAH: *(Fierce)* Bin dead.
(A smile) She bin a poor witch. I be much more talentet.

Act Two

MARY: Sarah hear things.

RUTH: Talket to her mama nightly. 'Tis verra peculiar.

DAME DOROTHY: We should leave this room.

RUTH: Time to rant yet, Sarah?

SARAH: Soon, soon.

DAME DOROTHY: Rant? What do you mean, rant?

(Little pause)

RUTH: Back to da kitchen. Da smella him maket me queasious, he gotta cheesy color inna face 'n' stinket sumpin wharfle.

MARY: *(Softly, looking at* DR BROWNE*)* Weep fer da travails a da flesh, fellow creatures. We bin all headet fer dat mordal day bed 'n' dat earfen hole.

RUTH: Soon…

*(*MARY *and* RUTH *exit.)*

DAME DOROTHY: He never meant to harm. You could carve that on his gravestone. He was never kind.
(To DR BROWNE*)* I've seen you feel…remorse. That's something. But…You did not live well upon this earth, Thomas.

*(*DAME DOROTHY *exits.* SARAH *lags behind.)*

BABBO: Verra. 'Tis not his fault he bin a stingy 'n' raptious blabbermouth, 'r' dat yer knacky ma got hanget.

SARAH: You watchet him good.

BABBO: You keepet yer hands offa my tarts 'n' chickens.

SARAH: All food belonget to all fellow creatures.

BABBO: Dat food fer aftah da funeral.

SARAH: Aftah da funeral, dey han't gonna feel much like eating.

BABBO: You don't know dese people. Dey will.

SARAH: Wait 'n' see. Dey han't gonna wanna eat.
(She goes.)

BABBO: Dose wimmin gonna snitch da nails outa da floorboards. Such a perturbet. Inna holden days, death bin a little do in da village a hanimals. Da moriens bin movet by da hoven fer warmth, 'r by a winda if dey had a fever 'n' wantet da coolth a da breezet. 'N' a soft moaning 'n' da tears flow, 'n' da world go on. Not hacta so perturbet, like da world bin ending, like today.

(THE ABBESS OF X crawls out from under the bed, across from where BABBO is sitting. BABBO sees her stand.)

BABBO: A hesprit!

(They regard each other.)

BABBO: Ah, hesprit, my old scaley eyes bin disconceiving me; you bin a phantasm in da pocket a my grief, 'r else you be da ghost a poor drownet Alice Browne. Can you speak?

THE ABBESS OF X: Babbo.

BABBO: You speaket...my name! Den you be da verra ghost a poor dear Alice. But tell me, hesprit, how come you bin dresset like a nun?

THE ABBESS OF X: Old woman. I was, I...am Alice Browne, but no ghost.

BABBO: Ah, nope? Bin you a vampire, 'r sumpin like dat, den?

THE ABBESS OF X: I'm not dead.

BABBO: Den you bin alive.

THE ABBESS OF X: Yes.

BABBO: Den you han't drownet on dat ship?

THE ABBESS OF X: No.

BABBO: But… We all thought you'd drownet.

THE ABBESS OF X: You were wrong.

(Pause)

BABBO: You gotta hexplanation?

THE ABBESS OF X: The ship sank. The sea was merciless. We had barely cleared Yarmouth harbor. Everyone on board perished, except myself.

BABBO: How bin you savet, Alice?

THE ABBESS OF X: I swam.

BABBO: Back ta Yarmouth?

THE ABBESS OF X: To France.

BABBO: You swam alla way to France!?

THE ABBESS OF X: Yes.

BABBO: But Alice, you han't know howta swim.

THE ABBESS OF X: I know. I was spared by the benevolent hand of God.

BABBO: *(Awestruck)* Verra?

THE ABBESS OF X: There were typhoons, Babbo, and great forked bolts of lightning, and fish with teeth! I thought my end had come. But I was rescued…by a vision.

BABBO: Sweet tootha da Virgin! A vision?

THE ABBESS OF X: An angel of God preceded me through the brine, dog-paddling. With an iron sword wrapped all in thorns and flaming hair.

BABBO: Red hair?

THE ABBESS OF X: *Flaming* hair, Babbo.
I learned to dog-paddle by emulating him, and when I grew too weary I clung to the hem of his heavenly raiment and he towed me to the beach at Boulogne.

BABBO: Well. Dat be sumpin, Alice.

THE ABBESS OF X: And on the beach the angel said, "Alice Browne, as you have clung to me, cling to the Holy and Apostolic Catholic Church, cleave to it, and in its clefts you will be safe from perils worse than drowning." I was summoned to turn my back on the great and perfidious Apostasy of my native land and seek, on foreign shores, the sweet succor of the One True Faith.

BABBO: But why han't you told us dat, Alice? Da doctah grievet long 'n' fulbous fer da lossa his sistah, 'n' we all did, 'n' whilst us weepet 'n' wet you bin a safet 'n' dry French nun. How come you han't write a letter, 'r sumpin'?

THE ABBESS OF X: Our order observes very strict rules of silence.

BABBO: Fer twenty years? What order be dat?

THE ABBESS OF X: I'm...not at liberty to say.

(DR BROWNE *stirs.*)

BABBO: He bin waket! Dr Browne! Look who swimmet da Channel just ta say good-bye.

THE ABBESS OF X: Babbo, hush! If...he saw me, the shock could kill him.

BABBO: He bin almost dead anyway.

THE ABBESS OF X: They mustn't know I've returned.

BABBO: Dey han't hold yer being a Catholic against you, Alice. Mrs Browne bin partial ta heretics; she yacket with three ranters inna kitchen at dis verra minute.

THE ABBESS OF X: I want to give my brother the Extreme Unction, Babbo. I want to try to wrench his wayward soul from the fires of Hell, from everlasting torment and utter damnation.

Act Two

BABBO: Well a course ya do, but how you gonna do dat?

THE ABBESS OF X: I have a special dispensation from the Archbishop of Anjou to perform last rites for Thomas. I must be at his side when the end comes; it's all a matter of timing.

BABBO: Have a seat, Alice, da wait won't be long.

(DR BROWNE *stirs again.*)

THE ABBESS OF X: The others will come and foul the plan. I need a disguise.

BABBO: Fer carnival last Shrove Tuesday Mrs Browne 'n' me sewet dis piggie suit fer da doctah ta wear. It bin a hoot. You wanna dresset like a pig, Alice? Dey nevah recognize ya. Dey thought Dr Browne bin a verra pig.

THE ABBESS OF X: But what would a pig be doing in Thomas's sickroom?

BABBO: Dere bin stranger 'n' dat in here already today 'n' it han't even noon yet.

THE ABBESS OF X: Too conspicuous.

BABBO: I gotta idea.

THE ABBESS OF X: Tell me.

BABBO: Inna village a my youf, whena body bin dying, dere was a old woman sit bya bed, 'n' she knittet da shroud outta soft wool with long bone needles. She bin a harbinger a death, 'n' her clacket sound bin heard all ovah da town. Clackety-clack.

DR BROWNE: (*From far off*) It is surprisingly deep here, and below the surface terribly cold, and the pull is treacherous. I am treading…

BABBO: Bin waket. Come with me, Alice. Don't die, Doctah, till we get back.

THE ABBESS OF X: Hurry.

(They go.)

DR BROWNE: *(Still far away)* Warm me, take me off to warmer lands on your dark timber ship.

(A strange figure, dressed in rags, enters, crosses to the bed. She wears a half-mask of an old, old woman and a black veil. All her clothes are black. It is DOÑA ESTRELITA, *disguised.)*

THE WASHER/DOÑA ESTRELITA: Thomas. Thomas, can you hear me?

DR BROWNE: *(Still far off)* Bake me in the sun, dry me in the arrid heat of your... *(He's out.)*

THE WASHER/DOÑA ESTRELITA: Already I bring warmth.

(She peels back the bedclothes and embraces him.)

THE WASHER/DOÑA ESTRELITA: Can you feel the heat of my heart, Thomas, of my blood?

DR BROWNE: Thank you, blest redeemer.

THE WASHER/DOÑA ESTRELITA: Be patient. You are split in two. You say yes, you say no. I come to purify.

(She slips away.)

DR BROWNE: The sun... *(He shudders)* ...clouds over...

(The lights change, the music begins, a lesser version of the false alarms in Act One.)

*(*DEATH *enters;* DR BROWNE *shudders violently. His* SOUL *sits up, the ladder doesn't appear.)*

HIS SOUL: The ladder... *(It sees* DEATH*)*
Good, let's get this over with.

DEATH: Thomas, we need to touch. You're very warm, fever...you burn for me.

HIS SOUL: He burns for you, I burn to leave—do it do it what are you waiting for?

Act Two

DEATH: I'm very sad. To kill this moment, it will never come again, and yet I ache to kill. I am so… *(He sniffs.)* so hungry… *(Sniffs again)* What's that smell?

HIS SOUL: Eat him! Crack his bones and suck the marrow!

DEATH: Delicious smell…
(He moves toward the door.)
Hot, moulten fruit. Crust puffing, browning. I wonder…what's cooking…in the kitchen.
A minute.
(He goes.)

HIS SOUL: No! Here! Come back! You fly, you flit, *you are too easily distracted!* It's amazingly difficult to end a life.

DR BROWNE: *(Opening his eyes)* Is he gone?

HIS SOUL: Fraud.

DR BROWNE: I used to do that as a child. The night men. Close your eyes, pull up the covers, count to ten and they go away. I cannot see that face again.
(Sits up, looks about) Was there a woman here? A dark Spanish woman? Did you see a…

HIS SOUL: I'm not your watchdog!

DR BROWNE: You're not my soul, either, just some malcontented noisy thing, a mere side-effect. Of the blockage.
(He strains to shit. Nothing. He's exhausted.)
It's all mine. What's in me is mine. My desire—

HIS SOUL: For everything but Paradise is yours.

DR BROWNE: My intellect—

HIS SOUL: The cesspool through which every pure and crystal thought is dragged, surfacing smeared with offal. Yours.

DR BROWNE: My writing.
(Pause)
Mine.

HIS SOUL: Ours.
I sang and your little sausage fingers twitched. Each note transcribed, from the grand high harmonics of Heaven, through me to you, through the clumsy and corruptible mechanisms of your hand to a wiggling pen dipped in black smut. Writing. Transcribed, transmogrified, everything you ingest winds up black smut, compost-producer.

DR BROWNE: If you really are my soul, it's inappropriate for you to despise me so luxuriously. I am your vessel.

HIS SOUL: My prison. And my one prison-pleasure: loathing you.

DR BROWNE: Why?

HIS SOUL: For writing. For murdering the song.

DR BROWNE: I recorded it for posterity!

HIS SOUL: "Posterity." I hate that word almost as much as I hate you. Immortality is what you'd like to say but can't, because you know—

DR BROWNE: Know what?

HIS SOUL: You betrayed me, you with your filthy little wishes and soiled little dreams and your innumerable, incomprehensible fears! I sang as angels do, golden lifting tones on an unending breath, floating music without inception or decline, music that makes a lie of time, a lie of death, of grief or loss or pain, music free of wall or membrane, top or bottom, direction, shape or meaning. I sang of Immortality and you—

DR BROWNE: Wrote something else.

HIS SOUL: Yes.

Act Two

(Little pause)

DR BROWNE: My words betrayed me. I wrote...what I did not mean to write. I saw the door of Heaven swing wide open, a miracle to see, but when I described what I saw inside, the room had changed, it...was rather empty, and...

*(*HIS SOUL *has gone.)*

DR BROWNE: Do you hear me? Hello!?
Pity me! You should! The world made me, the word betrayed me, I never wanted to see...
You'll be sorry...when I'm gone. You will.

*(*MACCABBEE *enters, hears* DR BROWNE *talking to himself.)*

MACCABBEE: Dr Browne?

DR BROWNE: Leave me alone. What do you want from me?

MACCABBEE: I stranglet dem chickens.

DR BROWNE: *(Horrified)* You... *What?*

MACCABBEE: Like you instructet. I stranglet dem poor chickens.

DR BROWNE: Well, what do you want me to do? Weep for them? Mourn for them? Why don't you just strangle me too, and let's end this farce, and Babbo can stuff me with persimmons and hazelnuts and roast me in the oven.

MACCABBEE: Dr Browne, you wannet me ta kill dem birds, 'n' now—

DR BROWNE: What were the results?

MACCABBEE: Well, before dey was pecking inna dirt 'n' sayet chicken words, 'n' aftah dey just lay still.

DR BROWNE: Clod! Ape! Answer my question! Did you weigh them?

MACCABBEE: Chicken A weighet three 'n' halfet pound before strangletation, 'n' aftah, three 'n' halfet pound. Chicken B weighet five pounds before, 'n' aftah weighet five pounds.

DR BROWNE: *(Calling out to his absent* SOUL*)* Do you hear that! Identical!

MACCABBEE: I know dat, I'm da one did da strangling. Chicken C weighet four pounds before I strangle it, 'n' aftah...
Weighet eight pounds.

DR BROWNE: Eight pounds?

MACCABBEE: Ah, yup.

DR BROWNE: It got...heavier?

MACCABBEE: Verra wirret, huh?

DR BROWNE: You're in error. Weigh it again.

MACCABBEE: Han't mistaket. I bin careful. Bin heavier.

DR BROWNE: IT CANNOT CONCEIVABLY WEIGH *MORE* DEAD THAN...

(BABBO *enters with* THE ABBESS OF X, *disguised as* THE WEAVER OF THE SHROUDS. *She wears a half-mask that transforms her into a frightening looking old woman, dressed in gray rags. She is virtually identical to the* THE WASHER, *as if they had bought their masks at the same shop.)*

BABBO: Secuse me, Doctah. Dis old lady wannet ta see if you bin inna market for a winding sheet—

DR BROWNE: Get her out of here!
(He is stricken with a terrible terrible pain in his gut.)
Oh mercy. What was that? Something...ripped.

THE WEAVER/THE ABBESS OF X: I bin a weaver a shrouds, Doctah Browne, I come from verra far away ta help out wif da unraveling.

DR BROWNE: I don't need help, I...

Act Two 45

Oh God, help. I think…I'm not doing well at all…oh.

MACCABBEE: Ya want me ta get a doctah, Doctah?

DR BROWNE: *(Pain!)* OH! OH!

MACCABBEE: I translate dat means yes.

THE WEAVER/THE ABBESS OF X: I'll just set up my knitting 'n' commencet da shroud. I only need da measurements.

(She approaches DR BROWNE with a measuring string. He recoils, completely terrified of her, and in horrible pain.)

DR BROWNE: No shroud! Leave!

THE WEAVER/THE ABBESS OF X: But Doctah, I bin reassuret; I knit, 'n' dah clicka my needles—

BABBO: 'N' da sayet a da psalms—

THE WEAVER/THE ABBESS OF X: 'N' da psalms, sure, bin verra reassuret. Now… *(Again with the string)* You know da twenny-third psalm, fer instance?

DR BROWNE: *(Physical agony, terror!)* NO CLICKS! NO PSALMS! Not for me you hyena, go prey on someone else's—

(DEATH enters, eating a chicken leg.)

DR BROWNE: *(Physical agony, much much more terror!!)* Oh, dear God. *You.* *(To* THE WEAVER*)* What was that psalm you mentioned?

THE WEAVER/THE ABBESS OF X: Da twenny-third.

DR BROWNE: Let's hear it.

(DR BROWNE lies back, still in horrible pain.)

THE WEAVER/THE ABBESS OF X:
Da Lord bin my shepert; I han't go wantet.
He make me restet inna green pastrahs,
He leadet me ta still watahs,
'N' restoret my soul.

(HIS SOUL *sits up.* DEATH *finishes the meat, chews the bone, licks his fingers.*)

THE WEAVER/THE ABBESS OF X: 'N' even ef I bin walket through da valley a da shadda a death, I fearet no hevil.

(DEATH *goes.* HIS SOUL *sinks.* MACCABBEE *enters with* DR DOGWATER.)

MACCABBEE: Here da doctah.

DR DOGWATER: Buh-Browne? I...Are you...oh my, you are. Guh-good people, the time has come, let us puh-puh-puh-pray.

(*He kneels, everyone kneels with him.*)

DR BROWNE: (*Very faint, very weak*) Maccabbee.

(MACCABBEE *goes to him.*)

DR BROWNE: This isn't the doctor I had in mind.

DR DOGWATER: Our f-father, who art in Heaven, look down, show mercy, on this, your wretched but faithful servant in his final hour, and show him the face of your eternal love—

BABBO: (*Simultaneously*) Dear Gawd, Dr Browne bin coming inta yer bosmet, 'n' dose of us who lovet him on earf ask you to hopen a place fer him in da hops a Heaven. He bin mostly a ceerible soul, got his faults like evahbody, 'n' you musset be used to faults, you made so many of dem—

MACCABBEE: (*Simultaneously, a bit louder than the others*) Our fathah who art in Heaven, fergive dose who trespasset against us. Uhh...I do not like thee, Dr Fell, I know not why, I cannot tell, but dis I know, 'n' know full well, I do not like thee, Dr Fell. I do not like thee, Dr Fell, oh bag a guts go burn in Hell, I—

(*Sotto voce, under the above hubbub,* THE ABBESS OF X *tries to sneak in the Extreme Unction, in Latin.*)

Act Two

DR DOGWATER: Wh-what was that?

(Silence)

DR DOGWATER: Duh-did I hear Luh-Latin?

(Silence. Still on his knees, DR DOGWATER walks toward THE ABBESS OF X.)

DR DOGWATER: Cuh-come on, I duh-did. Who was praying in Luh-Latin? You. Old wuh-woman.

THE WEAVER/THE ABBESS OF X: Ah, yoop?

DR DOGWATER: Who are you?

BABBO: She bin da shroud weaver, Dr Dogwater.

DR DOGWATER: She looks fah-fah-familiar. In a fuh-funny way. Cuh-come here.

(THE ABBESS OF X, on her knees, starts walking away from Dogwater, who, on his knees, pursues.)

(DAME DOROTHY rushes in, sees them kneeling.)

DAME DOROTHY: Oh my God, he's dead.

DR DOGWATER: Huh-he is?

(Everyone rushes to the bed to check.)

DR BROWNE: Not yet, but keep praying, I'm working on it.

(DR SCHADENFREUDE enters.)

DR SCHADENFREUDE: Move aside, move aside, you'll suffocate him.
(To DR DOGWATER) Please, sir, you're crowding my patient.

DR DOGWATER: He's *my* pah-pah-parishioner. Tuh-Thomas, I must speak, and in my vuh-voice you should hear not only muh-me, but the cuh-cuh-community of shareholders I represent, and your wuh-wife and your chuh-children—

DR BROWNE: Children! Dorothy did the children come? *(To* DR DOGWATER*)* Late as usual, late for everything, heel-draggers, lag-behinds—if they dawdle too much they'll miss my demise.

DAME DOROTHY: You wrote them such furious letters, summoning them. I'm sure they'll come.

(DR DOGWATER *tries to interject.*)

DR BROWNE: Half my children died in infancy. Those are the ones I loved. The others grew difficult. Their mother and I made thirteen of them.

DAME DOROTHY: Fourteen.

DR DOGWATER: Your children, whom you love tenderly, and—

DR BROWNE: Did they ever appreciate me? Ever show me gratitude? Ever produce grandchildren? HAH! The line comes to a dead halt. My eldest son. Michael. An honored member of the Royal Academy of Science. *My* experiments they never accepted; I'm told they await *his* reports eagerly. *I'm so proud.* He used to send copies to me, but then he…stopped.

DAME DOROTHY: *(Controlled fury)* You told him they were dull.

DR BROWNE: *(The same back at her)* They were.

DAME DOROTHY: *(The same back at him)* Well then, he stopped sending them. You got what you wanted.

DR DOGWATER: *(Exploding)* MUH-MAY I PUH-PLEASE FUH-FUH-FUH-FINISH!

(Silence)

DR DOGWATER: The Wuh-Will, Sir Thomas, I muh-must know where you puh-put it.

DR SCHADENFREUDE: I'd like to have a look at it myself, actually.

Act Two

DR DOGWATER: Y-you? May I ask whuh-why?

DR SCHADENFREUDE: Peruse the funeral arrangements. I want time to prepare.

DR DOGWATER: Prepare whuh-what?

DR SCHADENFREUDE: The eulogy.

DR DOGWATER: The eul-lah-lah…

DR SCHADENFREUDE: Eu-lo-gy.

DR BROWNE: Dorothy, please tell them all to go away.

DR DOGWATER: Wuh-wait. Am I to uh-understand that yuh-you are to be the eulogist at the fah-funeral? Y-*you*?

DR SCHADENFREUDE: I would imagine myself the likeliest candidate.

DR DOGWATER: Suh-Sir Thomas, is this indeed the cuh-case?

DR BROWNE: You can both eulogize me. Simultaneously. I won't have to listen.

DAME DOROTHY: It's time for everyone to leave. Now.

DR DOGWATER: Nuh-no. You disappoint me, Suh-Sir Thomas. Not only have you abrogated your fuh-financial committments, but now you intend to abdicate your suh-spiritual commitments as well and allow yourself to be eu-eu-eulogized by a duh-damned hack Heh-Hessian physician?

DR SCHADENFREUDE: *Hack?* You call me a *hack*?

DR DOGWATER: Wuh-well, Browne isn't suh-sterling evidence of your muh-medical competence, is he? Duh-doctors who know what they're duh-doing are usually suh-spared eulogizing their puh-patients.

DR SCHADENFREUDE: He wasn't killed by my treatments.

DR DOGWATER: He wasn't cuh-cured by them either.

DR SCHADENFREUDE: He probably grew that tumor sitting through too many fuh-fuh-four hour suh-suh-sermons, puh-puh-puh-Preacher.

(Deadly silence)

DR DOGWATER: *(Hurt, with dignity)* Duh-do you mock me? My ah-affliction? It doesn't injure me, n-not a buh-bit. I nuh-know that stupid, simple men like yourself suh-snigger behind my back. You say, "What good's a puh-preacher with a stuh-stutter?" You suh-sneer. But I remind you: Muh-muh-Moses stuttered. It is from God my stuh-stutter comes. With every huh-hitch and slip I fuh-feel his hot and angry love. Guh-God loves me. He loves my stuh-stutter. But what does he fuh-feel about *you*, Heh-Herr Doktor? Th-Thomas, this is what comes of your irresponsibility. I huh-hope you're puh-pleased.

(He leaves.)

DAME DOROTHY: Oh dear.

DR BROWNE: I seem to have lost center stage. May I make a small request?

DAME DOROTHY: What, Thomas?

DR BROWNE: I want a bath.
I am...astonishingly malodorous. A blossom of putrescence.

DR SCHADENFREUDE: I'd noticed. As though you'd begun to rot ahead of schedule.

DAME DOROTHY: No, Thomas, a bath would give you a chill.

DR BROWNE: I wouldn't mind a good shiver, one that comes from the temperature of water, rather than from...other things. I miss the little creature comforts:

Act Two

spring air, being thin, food, excrement. I would like a bath.

BABBO: You want I should get da sponge, Mrs Browne, 'n' da bastin?

DAME DOROTHY: You have other work to do.

BABBO: Ah, nope, da chickens been broastin and da tarts bin... *(She screeches.)* Doctah! Da tart!

DAME DOROTHY: Babbo please stop babbling about chickens and tarts, have some sense of occasion.

BABBO: But I put da...da tart in da hoven and in da tart dere was a...was a... *(She smacks herself in the head jar her memory.)*

DR BROWNE: Dorothy she's having a fit of some sort—

BABBO: Da Will! *I HID DA WILL IN DA—*

DR BROWNE: Sssshhh!

DAME DOROTHY: The Will? She hid the Will?

DR BROWNE: No, no, she means she "did my will"; the addled creature, her charming peasant patois, she's incomprehensible. Go forth, Babbo, and roast. Spice, mince, jolly, jolly.

(BABBO rushes out.)

DR BROWNE: Maccabbee!

MACCABBEE: You want me ta weigh Chicken C again?

DR BROWNE: Precisely.

MACCABBEE: I already hanticipate da houtcome. 'Tis verra wirret stoof.

(BABBO and MACCABBEE leave.)

DR BROWNE: I am going to bathe. In the river.

DR SCHADENFREUDE: I forbid it, Sir Thomas, there is still ice in the water, it's barely spring.

DR BROWNE: *(Trying to stand)* Help me up, Dorothy.

DAME DOROTHY: You want to die.

(DR BROWNE *stares at her.*)

DR BROWNE: Of course not.
Maybe not.
Maybe...I do.
Old woman, you help me.

THE WEAVER/THE ABBESS OF X: Ah no, Sir Thomas, da Lord ferbids us ta hasten da moment a our death. Ya haveta wait fer His hand. I han't help ya.

(THE WASHER/DOÑA ESTRELITA *enters.*)

DR BROWNE: It's my last request. Must I beg for everything?

THE WASHER/DOÑA ESTRELITA: No.

(*All turn to her.*)

THE WASHER/DOÑA ESTRELITA: Secuse da interruptet. I come ta help.
I preparet da moriens *(Mor-iens)*, I bin a washer a da dying and da dead. I purify. I bin sent fer.

DAME DOROTHY: Sent for by whom?

THE WASHER/DOÑA ESTRELITA: By him.

(*They look to* DR BROWNE, *who is staring hard at* THE WASHER.)

DAME DOROTHY: You're mistaken you have the wrong address.

THE WASHER/DOÑA ESTRELITA: Sir Thomas Browne.

DAME DOROTHY: He didn't send for a washer of corpses, he wouldn't, he's too afraid of...

THE WASHER/DOÑA ESTRELITA: 'N' you bin Dame Dorothy Browne, his wife. Please ta meetchoo. Now I taket him to da river fer his bath. You bin right, he bin

Act Two

verra much afraidet. Help him ta die, Missus, quench da fires dat sear him.

DAME DOROTHY: No! He doesn't...You're wrong.

THE WASHER/DOÑA ESTRELITA: Ast him yerself.

(Everyone looks at DR BROWNE *again. He nods.)*

DR BROWNE: I sent for her; she's come. She knows what I want, can't you hear that?

DAME DOROTHY: Thomas. Not yet.

DR BROWNE: I did not live well. That was true. I never intended harm. That was true.

DAME DOROTHY: You heard.

DR BROWNE: Tell the children...No. Don't tell them anything.

*(*DAME DOROTHY *leaves.)*

DR SCHADENFREUDE: Death's little cottage industries. Are you a vigorous scrubber?

THE WASHER/DOÑA ESTRELITA: Da skin glows where I scrubet; it blush 'n' glow.

DR SCHADENFREUDE: When my time comes, will you scrub for me?

THE WASHER/DOÑA ESTRELITA: Someone will.

DR SCHADENFREUDE: Thomas, enjoy your bath. Shall I have a servant carry him?

THE WASHER/DOÑA ESTRELITA: No need, I have strong arms.

*(*DR SCHADENFREUDE *leaves, smiling.)*

*(*THE WEAVER *gathers her things and starts to leave.)*

(At the last minute she throws a little holy water on DR BROWNE *and exits, muttering Latin.)*

DR BROWNE: *(Wiping water off his face)* The bath's already begun. How did I know you were coming to me? The ship, the warm seas...

THE WASHER/DOÑA ESTRELITA: Hush, don't try to understand.

DR BROWNE: Across the wide, calm, bathwater sea, pearly pink or moon-dappled, you sailed to me, to my deathbed, how mysterious, with candle-flickering eyes and cool, pale arms...

THE WASHER/DOÑA ESTRELITA: You never understood, Thomas.

DR BROWNE: I think now I never thought enough about love.

THE WASHER/DOÑA ESTRELITA: You never did. Come.

(She lifts him in her arms.)

THE WASHER/DOÑA ESTRELITA: Easy. To the river.

(They exit. His Soul sits up.)

HIS SOUL: *(Sings:)*
And do you love me, darling one?
To touch your face is lots of fun.
Your skin so clear and waist so trim:
"I cannot get enough of him!"
"I cannot get enough of her,
I want to eat the stuff of her!"
Ooh ah ooh ah,
The Heavens wheel and spin.
The Heavens wheel and spin.

And will you love me when I'm dead?
When hair and skin are off my head?
When bone is bared, and viscera,
Will you, my dear, still kisscera?
Oh will the little games we played
Still tempt us when we're both decayed?

Mortal love, mortal love,
Stabbed in the heart with mortal love.

Yesterday morn your breath was bad,
And truth to tell, it made me sad
To smell the hint upon that breath
Of the work of corruption
And the progress of Death.

(Intermission)

Act Three

THE DANCE OF DEATH

Glorious Golden Country Sunshine, Late Afternoon

(DR BROWNE's *bed is empty, as at the end of Act Two.*)
(MACCABBEE *enters, carrying a very swollen strangled Chicken C.*)

MACCABBEE: 'Tis a new age a scientiftic wondrament. Hemprical hobservations 'n' da careful hexamination a seemingly insignifticant phenomenas. Who knows where it all leadet? Dis chicken weighet three 'n' halfet pounds when it bin alive. Aftah death, it weighet eight pounds, like I told him. Now it weigh thirteen pounds. 'N' I suspeck 'n' predick it han't done haccumulating mass, neiver.

(*He puts the strangled chicken on* DR BROWNE's *pillow*)
I leavet here 'n' he can see fer himself, when he bin finishet wif his baptism.

(*Little pause*)

I wanna die inna grand style, wif a sense of pompet 'n' circumfrence, but I bin probably gonna die hignominious, all loathesome 'n' wacket a da clap inna poorhouse hovel. He coulda hadda nicet kind a death, he got da money fer it, but he always bin knacky. Evah readet one a his books? I tried, oncet. I han't followet da narrative. Strucket me as hover-written.

(HIS SOUL's *voice is heard.*)

HIS SOUL: You! Amanuensis! Hireling! Water boy!

MACCABBEE: A voicet! *(He turns around.)* A disembloodet voicet! *Verra* creepet. Must be a hecho. *(Turns back)*

HIS SOUL: MACCABBEEEEEEEE!

(MACCABBEE *turns again.* HIS SOUL *rises slowly.*)

MACCABBEE: Wirret. A miniscule homunculus. Who you be, babbie, da toof fairy?

HIS SOUL: I'm...I'm Browne's soul.

MACCABBEE: Aw, hang dat up ta dry. You han't his soul. He han't got one.

HIS SOUL: He'd like to believe that, but here I am, a casualty of his crisis of faith.

MACCABBEE: Ef you bin da verra soul a Browne, how come you han't down by da rivah, watching him get washet by dat knacky old bat he sent fer?

HIS SOUL: I expected to go with him, like before, but there was only a tug. You...you see me

MACCABBEE: Hobviously.

HIS SOUL: Something's wrong. He ought to be dead soon, and I should be well-nigh to weightless, but... *Touch me.*

MACCABBEE: What fer?

HIS SOUL: Just...the tip of my finger. Just a quick touch.

(MACCABBEE *does it.* HIS SOUL *draws back in horror and disgust.*)

HIS SOUL: Oh God! How revolting!

MACCABBEE: Dat's a mighty shitten thing ta say. Han't you got manners?

Act Three

HIS SOUL: Oh God you *touched* me. I've been *touched*.

MACCABBEE: Calm yerself, ya han't catch it just by touching.

HIS SOUL: Catch what?

MACCABBEE: Da clap.

HIS SOUL: The...?
Oh God, I've become...*meat*. Oh god I have a *skin*. Oh, but that's imposs...
The *clap*. What's *"the clap"*?

MACCABBEE: A venereal hinfection. A disease constracted by fornicating hindiscriminately.

HIS SOUL: I feel sick.

MACCABBEE: Well how ya think I feel? It consumet my nose. It's a harful hembarrassment. Dis bronze prophylactus han't foolet no one, though it bin more decorative dan a wood one, don't ya think?

HIS SOUL: Kill him.

MACCABBEE: Secuse me?

HIS SOUL: Kill him! Browne! Kill kill kill him! He has to die soon! Look, look at me!

MACCABBEE: You look okay. A little wirret, but...

HIS SOUL: You shouldn't be able to look at me at all! I'm METAPHYSICAL! Three weeks ago even *he* couldn't see me, and now I'm being *fingered* by his manservant. I'm doomed unless he dies! I want to climb! Save me, kill the bastard—it's your duty as a Christian.

MACCABBEE: I dunno, dat be hard ta sell ta a judge 'n' jury.

HIS SOUL: I'll give you something.

MACCABBEE: Like what, fer instance?

HIS SOUL: Well, like…oh anything, WHATEVER, I don't care.

MACCABBEE: I'll do it if ya get inna bed with me.

HIS SOUL: If I do…*what*?

MACCABBEE: I han't ever made it with a metaphysical hactuality before.

HIS SOUL: I'll burn in Hell first.

MACCABBEE: Ah, yoop. Well, lemme think. You bin going ta Heaven aftah he dies?

HIS SOUL: Yes! Heaven! If he dies soon!

MACCABBEE: When you arrivet in Heaven, talket to da Blesstet Virgin 'r someone with charitable hinclinations. Rid me a da clap. Bringet back my nose.

HIS SOUL: I couldn't…guarantee anything, of course, but I…might…

MACCABBEE: Ef ya gimme yer wordet, I kill him onna gamble.

HIS SOUL: You'd kill your master on a *gamble*?

MACCABBEE: It bin sumpin I always wannet ta do anyway. 'N' ef it gets me a miraculous restoration on my nose, so much da more da merrier, 'tis what I say.

HIS SOUL: Deal. But nothing painful, and…try not to enjoy it too much. *(Looking upward)* Forgive me, Father, I don't know what I'm doing. Well, I do know, but… Oh God, *skin, meat, blood*, oh help me, help me, I think I'm starting to…to *smell*…

(HIS SOUL *vanishes as* BABBO *enters, splotchy with various fruit jellies.*)

BABBO: I bin distresset. I searchet through evah one a dem hot baket tarts, 'n' I hant find da one with dat papah. Maybe it burnet hup.

Act Three

MACCABBEE: I gotta a remedy fer when things feelet upset-down.

BABBO: What?

(They look at each other.)

BABBO: *Now?*

MACCABBEE: 'N' look! Da bed bin unoccupied.

BABBO: Ah, nope, not dere, da linens on dat bed bin soilet to da verra point a crawling.

MACCABBEE: It's da smella weariness 'n' fear. Maket me wanna do da Molloch.

BABBO: Probably a mordal sin... Ah, well, I gotta coupla minnits.

(They hop into bed and begin to fuck. DAME DOROTHY enters, carrying a candle; MACCABBEE throws the covers over them just in time and they lie very still, but Chicken C is left lying atop the bedclothes. DAME DOROTHY goes to the desk and begins searching through the papers. MACCABBEE sits up, tosses Chicken C behind the headboard and goes back under the covers.)

DAME DOROTHY: Oh why bother searching? He obviously didn't write a Will. Punish the world for continuing after, keep everyone worrying until he's gone: it would be so like Thomas to die intestate.

(From her bodice she produces a document looking very much like the document DR BROWNE gave BABBO in Act One. She looks to make sure she's alone, then reads it, audibly, but to herself.)

DAME DOROTHY: "I Sir Thomas Browne being of sound mind etcetera etcetera etcetera do hereby bequeath etcetera etcetera all my shares in the Walsingham Quarry to my beloved wife Dame Dorothy etcetera..."

(She goes to DR BROWNE's desk, places the fake Will in the desk drawer. PUMPKIN enters with a corpse wrapped in a

shroud. She doesn't hear him. He drops the corpse on the floor near her. She spins, badly startled.)

PUMPKIN: Afternoon, Dorfy.

(She sees the corpse and screams.)

PUMPKIN: 'Tis a client a mine.

DAME DOROTHY: Oh mercy, I thought it was Thomas.

PUMPKIN: Ah, nope, bin some poor old sot dey give me ta bury inna pauper's field. I bringet him to da German doctah in hexchange fer a nominous recompensideration.

(DAME DOROTHY bends close to the corpse to see it more clearly, holding her candle. When she gets too close, the candle flares wildly!! DAME DOROTHY jumps back.)

PUMPKIN: Could you put out dat candle, Dorfy?

(DAME DOROTHY blows out the candle.)

PUMPKIN: Thanks, da earfly remains a dis doof bin so fulla gin and cheap brandy combustiples a spark might hignite a hexplosion.

DAME DOROTHY: Could we...could you put him somewhere? Under the bed, or...it's unnerving.

PUMPKIN: Ah, yup. Secuset.

(He stows the corpse under the bed.)

PUMPKIN: A man gotta be henterprising. Han't catchet me passing by a chance ta supplement my yearning.

DAME DOROTHY: You're an ambitious man, Leonard.

PUMPKIN: You still bin broodet, my love.

DAME DOROTHY: I...I've made a difficult decision, Leonard. I have to tell you something.
(Little pause)

Act Three

I am going to be the owner of the quarry, Leonard, when Thomas dies. Of the Walsingham fields, of the quarry, of this house and estate—

PUMPKIN: 'N' a gross heapet horde inna bank.

DAME DOROTHY: Yes. I was looking for the Will, to make sure everything's in order, because…I have plans, Leonard.
When Thomas is dead, and a proper amount of time has passed, I want to marry you, Mr Pumpkin.

PUMPKIN: Be Dorfy Pumpkin den, 'n' not a Dame 'r nuffin. But ef we growet rich enough dey might knight me someday.

DAME DOROTHY: And after we marry…
And then I intend to make Walsingham Fields common land again. Open to cottagers, smallholders.

PUMPKIN: For rent.

DAME DOROTHY: No rent. Free, common lands. Close down the quarry, let the grass grow over it, water fill it, cover the machines, the scars. In ten years time it will be as though it had never existed.

(Pause)

PUMPKIN: Dorfy—

DAME DOROTHY: And you and I will have a cottage there, and live poor but happy existences growing what we need and praying to God for forgiveness. Oh, Leonard, I know you wanted wealth but believe me, I know what wealth is and—

PUMPKIN: You know what, Dorfy? You ent actually know nuffin. What dis about, huh? Bin a test ta see ef I lovet, ta see ef I be true without da money, bin dat?

DAME DOROTHY: No, Leonard, it's my…it's what I want, Leonard.

PUMPKIN: Well, den fuck whatchoo want, cause dat be da knackiest 'n' stupidest shit I ever sat 'n' listet to.

DAME DOROTHY: Leonard—

PUMPKIN: Common lands. Whatchoo know about dat? I bin a boy onna commons—I watchet teef fall out 'n' hair turn gray onna heads a da young. I seen da men 'n' wimmin actet like beasten, act like da dumb ox 'n' da beatet dog, crushet by da heavy hand a no idea what dere be in dis world, dat dere bin more ta hexistence dan birth 'n' grief 'n' bitter death. 'N' I see da rich go by in deir silk 'n' gold 'n' jewelet, like high dark angels dat inhabitet another earf, where you han't no hope cause you bin stucket inna common lands by Gawd. But I left. 'N' thanks fer da invitation, Dame Dor-o-fy, but I han't going back.

DAME DOROTHY: We could share. Make common cause with the other cottagers, like the ranters say.

PUMPKIN: Dere bin no more ranters, Dorfy. Dey bin squashet by da bishops years ago, 'n' dem three hoors ya taket in bin eiver deludet, 'r lying, 'r both. Oncet dere bin thousands rantet. 'N' shaket 'n' quaket 'n' level 'n' dig. Say no rent, say food from da heavens, 'n' even though I bin a boy den I knew it bin crap, bin fairy stories 'n' farts inna wind. 'N' now dem voicet ent heard from no more. We gotta get on with da bloodet business a making do. I digget graves fer da rich 'n' poor. Da rich pay better but I han't say which I enjoy da most ta dig. 'N' before dey dig a grave fer me, I gonna be rich. 'N' dat be with you, Dorfy, 'r not. You throw out what most folks never had.

(Pause)

DAME DOROTHY: Ten miles from here there is the highway. People sleep on the open road at night. On cold mornings there's some who don't wake up. You see them, ice-crusted...I want a thicker skin but

Act Three

it won't grow. At night I hear those machines in the quarry pounding and I think: it's flesh those hammers pound, it's bone. We're immensely rich but we live without luxury. He can't bear to part with anything, even remorse, and I can't bear the accumulation. Thomas is lucky to die. I must live on here for a while yet, and I hate this life. In me there is a bleeding wound, and it never heals, and it's full of blood, and full of light, and there's paradise in there, besieged and unreachable but always beckoning. And the more foul and ugly the world becomes the more it beckons. The more it aches.

I can't live like this, Leonard, I have to do something.

PUMPKIN: When da doctah bin dead, Dorfy, 'n' I dug his grave...we talket summore. Do nuffin till den. Alright?

I love you, Dorfy.

DAME DOROTHY: Promise me, Leonard: tell my plans to no one. Promise.

PUMPKIN: Ah, yup. Come to da woods. I wanna soothe yer yeart.

DAME DOROTHY: My heart needs that.

Are you with me, Leonard?

PUMPKIN: Right now I be.

(They look at each other, then exit silently. MACCABBEE *sticks his head up, then* BABBO.*)*

MACCABBEE: How about dat?

BABBO: Da missus bin swoggling da gravedigger.

MACCABBEE: Him dying maket her hotter 'n him living ever did.

BABBO: I wanna leavet. I gotta find dat tart...
(Hearing something) Hisst!

(They throw the covers over themselves again, as DR DOGWATER *enters. He looks about, making sure he's alone, then removes from an inner pocket a fake Will. He skim-reads.)*

DR DOGWATER: "I Sir Thomas B-B-Browne, being of sound mind and buh-body...do by this instrument deed all my shuh-shares in the Walsingham Quarry to Luh-Luh-Leviticus Duh-Dogwater, D. Duh-D.... In ah-appreciation of..." buh-buh-blah and so forth. We promise You, uh-Almighty God, we will cuh-continue to search every nuh-nook and cranny for the ruh-real Will, but...Fuh-forgive us our fuh-forgeries as we forgive those who fuh-fuh-forge against us.

(He puts the Will in the Bible, when suddenly he hears someone coming and runs to the bed. He almost dives under the bedclothes, then at the last minute he sniffs the linens and changes his mind, hiding instead behind the drapes.)

*(*THE WEAVER/THE ABBESS OF X *enters and begins to search through the papers on the desk.)*

*(*DR DOGWATER *jumps out and surprises her.)*

DR DOGWATER: It's a fuh-fuh-flogging offense at the very least, burglary.

THE WEAVER/THE ABBESS OF X: AH! Oh, oh please, Pastah, han't callet da authorities, I was only...uh... looking fer my needles. I lost dem in dis pile a papah.

DR DOGWATER: Do you think I'm a fuh-fool? Your story is tuh-transparently false. You're a cuh-common thief and you nuh-need a good fuh-fuh-flogging. This way, please.

(He grabs her roughly by the arm. She executes a perfect karate flip and drops him to the floor.)

THE WEAVER/THE ABBESS OF X: Oops. Sorry, Pastah, dat was a hinvoluntary reflex.

Act Three

DR DOGWATER: *(Scrambling to his feet)* How duh-duh-dare you?

THE WEAVER/THE ABBESS OF X: *(Dropping into a fighting stance)* Ah, Pastah, han't be wise ta fight wif me, I bin verra dangerous.

DR DOGWATER: *(Circling in)* Dangerous! The duh-day I'm unable to best an old crone in a test of phuh-physical prowess is the day I...

(She lunges, jabs him sharply in the guts, spins, chops him in the neck, and kicks him in the ass. He goes sprawling.)

THE WEAVER/THE ABBESS OF X: I warnet you.

DR DOGWATER: You're nuh-no shuh-shroud weaver.

(Pause)

THE WEAVER/THE ABBESS OF X: No.

DR DOGWATER: In the nuh-name of God, who are you?

THE WEAVER/THE ABBESS OF X: I bin someone you knew verra well, oncet.

DR DOGWATER: I thought you were familiar. Who...

(She removes her disguise.)

THE ABBESS OF X: Hello, Leviticus.

DR DOGWATER: Ah, nuh-no, it cuh-cuh-can't be y... Ah-ah-ah-ah—

THE ABBESS OF X: Alice.

DR DOGWATER: Then where have you buh-been, oh Alice, where have—

THE ABBESS OF X: I was almost your bride once, Leviticus. A long time ago. Now you see me, a bride of Christ.

DR DOGWATER: A wh...? A *nah-nah-nah-NUN?!*

THE ABBESS OF X: An abbess.

DR DOGWATER: A cah-cah-Catholic nah-nah-nah—

THE ABBESS OF X: Ave Maria, Leviticus, et pax vobiscum.

DR DOGWATER: When you d...d...Alice, when the shipwreck, when I huh-heard, I was inconsolable, Alice. I foreswore puh-pleasure and my thoughts turned Heavenward, for suh-suh-suh—

THE ABBESS OF X: For succor.

DR DOGWATER: In your memory I dedicated my life to His service. And in God I found suh-sweetness surpassing, but only by a luh-little, the sweetness I'd known with you.
And now God torments me by returning you to me, a muh-minion of the antichrist in ruh-Rome, a rag of the buh-buh-beast.

THE ABBESS OF X: The One True Church. And you, Leviticus, a lieutenant schismatic.

DR DOGWATER: It's a good thing I'm not disposed to despair. I assume, Alice, that as a nah-nun, you now subscribe to the uh-unnatural puh-practice of celibacy?

THE ABBESS OF X: I must request that you cease to address me by my former name. Alice Browne perished in that shipwreck. In Christ's Church she was reborn, and by His vicar on earth she was rebaptised.

DR DOGWATER: And to what name does she cuh-currently answer?

THE ABBESS OF X: Mother Magdalena Vindicta, of the Abbey of X.

DR DOGWATER: Aix-en-Provence? Puh-pretty town, I vuh-visited it once in my travels.

THE ABBESS OF X: No, not Aix. X. The Abbey of X.

DR DOGWATER: I suh-said Aix.

THE ABBESS OF X: Not A-I-X. Just X.

DR DOGWATER: X.

THE ABBESS OF X: Just...X.

DR DOGWATER: And where, pray tell, is that?

THE ABBESS OF X: I'm not at liberty to say. In the first flush of my newfound faith I joined the Discalced Carmelites, but I found them too French, not strict enough. Then over the years I learned of other British nuns, expatriates, and we banded together—the sole survivors of our fatherland's spiritual collapse.

DR DOGWATER: I object to that.

THE ABBESS OF X: We laughed and wept as God smote your Apostasy with pestilence worse than the Egyptian plagues. And finally we decided to take a hand...

DR DOGWATER: A hand in what?

THE ABBESS OF X: We trained for years in Sicily. The bloody arts, unfit, some might say, for women: violence, poison and war. And we became adepts. Of great precision and skill.

DR DOGWATER: Wh-what are you tuh-talking about?

THE ABBESS OF X: The death of Cromwell, for example.

DR DOGWATER: A nuh-natural death.

THE ABBESS OF X: If you call belladonna natural, yes.

DR DOGWATER: Are you suh-saying that you ah-assassinated Cuh-Cromwell?

THE ABBESS OF X: My predecessor did. And the last two archbishops of Canterbury. We have their hats hanging on the wall of our refectory.

DR DOGWATER: Thuh-this is monstrous. I don't believe you.

THE ABBESS OF X: We will not rest until we've driven the last vestiges of the False Creed out of England.

DR DOGWATER: And you ruh-really expect to do that? One little cuh-convent full of addled nuns?

THE ABBESS OF X: It's a beginning.

DR DOGWATER: Y-you're completely insane, Alice. The Church of England is the Church of the fuh-fuh-future. No one wants Cah-Catholicism back. We duh-don't sell indulgences now, we sell cuh-cuh-commodities! The tide of history—

THE ABBESS OF X: God's truth knows no history! The Mysteries of the Faith aren't subservient to market fluctuations! A true servant of Christ is not shaken by surface changes in worldly affairs. We are entering a time of great tribulation when men strive to have pierced the Cloud of Unknowing, to have stripped the veil from the face of God. And what horrors will that not unleash? But the Church, Leviticus, is built on a rock and will withstand the firestorm, while your wretched and compromised adaptation stands only on a shifting pile of cash—and the winds will scatter it, the whole ragbag scrapheap.

DR DOGWATER: God will dispose of us as He sees fit, and adaptability is His wuh-way. With a buh-breath of his nostrils He suh-swept away your cloud, and let me tell you suh-something, Alice, nuh-no one misses it. We want light, not dah-dah-darkness. Plain words, not Luh-Latin blather. Your priests are fuh-fat. I'm not fuh-fat. I don't buh-bathe my flesh in wine and milk, I suh-swim in fuh-freezing ponds. Harsh, but solid! My faith has an industrial vitality. Work for Christ! Accumulate! Accumulate! That's my cuh-credo!

THE ABBESS OF X: They should never have translated the Bible. You are the crippled progeny of that labor.

Act Three

DR DOGWATER: Why did you come back?

THE ABBESS OF X: My brother will die a Catholic.

DR DOGWATER: Over my d...over my d...my d...like Hell he will. He's a puh-professed Protestant.

THE ABBESS OF X: A mere technicality.

DR DOGWATER: If his soul is all you're concerned about, why are you ruh-rifling through his thuh-things? Luh-looking for something? Puh-perhaps the luh-last Will and Testament. Perhaps not so unconcerned with muh-money after all.

THE ABBESS OF X: Our abbey needs funds, Leviticus. An endowment would be a blessing, spare us from soliciting contributions through...other methods.

DR DOGWATER: I shall reveal this to Thomas when he returns.

THE ABBESS OF X: You loved me once.

DR DOGWATER: Wuh-once I did. But the woman I loved is d...

THE ABBESS OF X: Dead. Then we are enemies.

DR DOGWATER: Unalterably and uh-irrevocably. Your buh-brother will suh-spurn you, you won't get a cent.

THE ABBESS OF X: We'll see. He was never one of you. He's not so well scrubbed. His books are very strange.

DR DOGWATER: I nuh-never liked them. But at heart, Thomas is suh-suh-solid. A buh-business-minded man. A suh-scientist.

THE ABBESS OF X: A scientist. When we were children, he tried to learn to track and plot the stars. Maps, charts, astronomy, a new science. But night after night he would sit in the grass and gaze up at the sky, mouth and eyes wide open, and shiver at the immensity, the immeasurability, the profound depth of Heaven. The charts lay idle, soaking up the night dew gathering in the grass. He was never a scientist.

He'll help his sister. I shall pray for it.

DR DOGWATER: Puh-pray all you like! God's fuh-forgotten Latin! He won't understand a wuh-word!

(She begins to exit, then suddenly performs another spectacular martial arts maneuver, knocking Dogwater flat. She pulls a fake Will from her wimple, stuffs it under the pillow on the bed, gathers up her disguise and exits.)

DR DOGWATER: *(Still flat out, in pain)* Was that ruh-really necessary?

*(*MACCABBEE *sneaks out of the bed and exits.* DR SCHADENFREUDE *enters.* DR SCHADENFREUDE *watches* BABBO, *who is sneaking out of bed. She exits as* DR DOGWATER, *unseeing, from the floor, says:)*

DR DOGWATER: *(Rising, wincing in pain, not seeing yet that* THE ABBESS OF X *is gone)* You wuh-wrenched my back!

*(*DR DOGWATER *limps to the family Bible to check on his Will.)*

DR SCHADENFREUDE: *(Gleeful)* Searching for lost souls, perhaps?

*(*DR DOGWATER *turns, startled.)*

DR SCHADENFREUDE: Find the Will yet?

DR DOGWATER: That duh-doesn't concern you.

DR SCHADENFREUDE: It does. I want to be Sir Thomas's eulogist. It's only fitting: we were both men of science, I stewarded him through his final illness and did it well, regardless of your low opinion of my procedures. It means a lot to me.

DR DOGWATER: I have a nagging suspicion you aren't muh-motivated exclusively by fah-fah-fraternal affections.

Act Three

DR SCHADENFREUDE: His Majesty the King will be in attendance at the funeral.

DR DOGWATER: I nuh-know. What can that puh-possibly mean to you?

DR SCHADENFREUDE: The office of Court Physician, I hear, is open.

DR DOGWATER: I duh-doubt that they'll want the position fuh-filled by a juh-German. No offense.

DR SCHADENFREUDE: *(Smiling, happy)* None taken. I have a letter of recommendation to the king from his cousin the elector of Hanover.

DR DOGWATER: Then why don't you just guh-go to Luh-London with your letter? What are you duh-doing here?

DR SCHADENFREUDE: I arrived in London in 1649, precisely on the day of Charles the First's decapitation. A king without a head…

DR DOGWATER: Duh-doesn't need a doctor.

DR SCHADENFREUDE: *(Amused)* JA! I settled here, in Norfolk, where I could be inconspicuous.

(DR DOGWATER *gives him a look.*)

DR SCHADENFREUDE: And now with the crown secure on the royal head and the royal head secure on the rest of the royal body my desire to serve His Majesty prompts me forward. What better way to make an impression than with a gripping eulogy for a highly esteemed artist and monarchist? It's the least I'm owed for my services.

DR DOGWATER: Dr Schadenfreude, I am the puh-prelate for this parish, and huh-highly trained, and I will give the eulogy. You'll have to look elsewhere for a ruh-rostrum for your tuh-tuh-tawdry political mah-mah-machinations.

(DR SCHADENFREUDE *pulls off a glove and slaps* DR DOGWATER!)

DR SCHADENFREUDE: *(Echt Prussian!)* Dogwater, I challenge you to a duel.

DR DOGWATER: A duel? You expect a man of God to fuh-fight a duel?

DR SCHADENFREUDE: *(Wielding his walking stick like a fencing foil)* JA! Of *words*! Your eulogy against mine! Let each applicant for the position commit his text to memory! And then let Browne decide!

(DR DOGWATER *shakes the end of the walking stick, which has been pointed at his chest, in grim agreement.*)

(THE WASHER/DOÑA ESTRELITA *enters, carrying* DR BROWNE *wrapped in a blanket.*)

DR DOGWATER: Huh-he's buh-back.

(She places him in the bed.)

DR SCHADENFREUDE: Did he enjoy his bath? Or did it kill him?

THE WASHER/DOÑA ESTRELITA: Bin livet still, but bin verra close to da end.

DR DOGWATER: Buh-Browne? Can you hear me? The Will, Browne, the Wuh-Will!

DR BROWNE: *(Deep in a blissful, sexy dream)* …in tunnels underneath…

DR DOGWATER: Tuh-tunnels?

DR BROWNE: …buried deep…

DR DOGWATER: The Will? You buh-buried the Will?

DR BROWNE: Yes. By the river. Deep.

DR DOGWATER: He buh-buried it! By the rah-river! Oh God, I am beset from all suh-sides. Where can I get a shovel?

Act Three

(He rushes out.)

DR BROWNE: *(Luscious, sensual, happy)* Tunnels by the river. Large, black velvet, muscular moles. With formidable claws and paddle paws and tough little cartilage-blunt stubbins for noses, blind blind blind blind blind…Estrelita?

DR SCHADENFREUDE: Estrelita?

DR BROWNE: Doña Estrelita…

(He sinks entirely into sleep.)

DR SCHADENFREUDE: Who is Doña Estrelita, Browne?

(DOÑA ESTRELITA sheds her disguise; under her weaver rags and mask she is a spectacular Spanish noblewoman, dressed to the nines.)

DOÑA ESTRELITA: I am.

DR SCHADENFREUDE: And who are you? Really?

DOÑA ESTRELITA: Doña Estrelita Maria Luz Angelica Brava y Gambon. The wife of the Spanish ambassador to the court of Charles II.

DR SCHADENFREUDE: You're the wife of the Sp…and this washing business, something you do for a lark?

DOÑA ESTRELITA: A small deception to gain access. Decades ago I loved this man. No one knows how much.
I've come to help him die. And take him home, to Spain, with me.

DR SCHADENFREUDE: To Spain?

DOÑA ESTRELITA: I can't bear the thought of him resting in this swampsoil, dissolving. Years ago I gave him up to the suction of this marshy island. In death, at last, I will have him with me, in the crucible land, the desert land of sand and dry ash, in Spain.

DR SCHADENFREUDE: I'm flattered that you chose to reveal yourself to me, great lady.

DOÑA ESTRELITA: Fellow foreigner.

DR SCHADENFREUDE: I am a student of the world's variety and I have observed... There are many kinds of lovers. Some sunlit and happy. Some moonstruck and griefstricken.

DOÑA ESTRELITA: And some driven by curious passions, pallid, silent, drawn to the dark.

(DOÑA ESTRELITA *and* DR SCHADENFREUDE *stare at each other with an icy fervor.*)

DR SCHADENFREUDE: We are, I suspect, kindred spirits, Doña.

DOÑA ESTRELITA: You are from the cold north, Doctor. I am from the hot south. It's the people in the middle I don't trust.

DR SCHADENFREUDE: And how, most charming lady, do you plan to accomplish this crypt robbing? You won't get him out the front door.

DOÑA ESTRELITA: *(Hearing a noise)* Someone's coming! My disguise!

(MACCABBEE *enters, carrying a huge urn.* DOÑA ESTRELITA *hides in the curtains.*)

MACCABBEE: Da urn arrivet. Bin dead?

DR SCHADENFREUDE: What have we here?

(DR SCHADENFREUDE *examines the urn,* MACCABBEE *goes to the bed.* HIS SOUL *appears.*)

HIS SOUL: You have to do it soon! I've become so *thick*!

MACCABBEE: My nose, remembah!

HIS SOUL: SOON!

Act Three

MACCABBEE: *(Searching the bedclothes)* You seen dat chicken, Doctah Schadenfreude?

(HIS SOUL *reaches behind the headboard and throws* MACCABBEE *the chicken, swollen even larger than at the top of the scene.* HIS SOUL *sinks from view.)*

MACCABBEE: Here 'tis. Gawd, I gotta weigh dis bird again. It bin positively collostal.
(He goes with the chicken.)

DR SCHADENFREUDE: He's gone.
Doña Estrelita, he's gone.
Dona Estrelita?

(She crawls out.)

DOÑA ESTRELITA: *(Delighted)* There's a body under this bed.

DR SCHADENFREUDE: *(Looking)* A spare! Redolent of Barbados rum!

DOÑA ESTRELITA: Is there a large oven in the house?

DR SCHADENFREUDE: In the kitchen.

DOÑA ESTRELITA: I want to have a look. I gotta plan.

(They exit.)

(DEATH *enters, eating a tart. He bites down on something unexpected and removes from the tart* DR BROWNE's *Will. Placing the tart on* DR BROWNE's *bed,* DEATH *opens it, reads and chuckles.)*

DEATH: *(Striking a pose for declaiming poetry, one foot forward, one hand behind his back:)*
Unsound, thy body;
unstrung, thy mind,
and yet thou leave'st thy Will behind.

(DEATH *pockets the Will. He raises his knife, walks toward* DR BROWNE, *ready to kill, then stops, uncertain.)*

(SARAH *enters.)*

DEATH: I'm very...unhappy.

SARAH: Hoosh, babbie, I knowet.

DEATH: It's like sharp nettles. I frighten him. He doesn't love me. I want his love. I want to rip his heart out and eat it. *(He raises his knife to strike.)*

SARAH: Soon, babbie, soon...I gotta little do ta do, firstet.

*(*DEATH *moves a step or two toward Sarah. She is very frightened of him, but holds her ground.)*

DEATH: It's the appetite that never dies. The body dies. The mind dies. The heart stops beating. EVERYTHING DROPS AWAY! But this sharp painful hunger lingers on.

SARAH: Dancet wif me, babbie. It taket yer mind off da ache.

*(*DEATH *approaches her, she backs away at first, involuntarily recoiling from him. Then she takes his proffered hand. They dance slowly as* HIS SOUL *sings.)*

HIS SOUL: *(Singing:)*
The lamb of God is bleating,
Heaven help the stupid thing!
For the daylight is retreating
And the owl is on the wing.

On the wing the hungry owl;
There is murder on the wind;
And the wolf is on the prowl;
And a scent is in the air...

A bloody teardrop rolling
From its gold reproachful eye:
Thou hast I think forsook thy lamb
And no more hear its cry:

Crying pity and despair;
For a scent is in the air;

And there's murder in the wind;
And the wolf is on the prowl;
Oh forgive me, I have sinned;
On the wing, the hungry owl...

(The other ranters enter. DEATH *bows,* SARAH *curtsies. He kisses her hand and leaves. As the song concludes the ranters surround* DR BROWNE's *bed.)*

HIS SOUL: Ah, faith.
It is amazing.
And the night is dark and chill,
And the little lamb is grazing
On a clover-covered hill.
And the stars are blotted out
By the cold and distant moon
And the night grows darker still;
Pray for daybreak.
Make it soon.

(Intermission)

Act Four

WHO SEES GOD'S FACE, THAT IS SELF LIFE, MUST DIE

Fiery Apocalyptic Sunset, Early Evening

(DR BROWNE *is alone, sleeping on his bed. The ranters surround him, watching.*)

(SARAH *makes a gesture and the lights in the room dim and change.*)

SARAH: Dere bin always a time a reckoning, Browne, a counting a da stores 'n' a parceling out, 'n' dat time come fer you at last. 'Tis now fer da rant 'n' da curset, fellow creatures. Helpet 'n' make dis loafa bad bread ready fer da doings, whilst I preparet myself.

(SARAH *undresses.* MARY *and* RUTH *undress* DR BROWNE *and hoist him, unconscious, to his feet.* DR BROWNE *and* SARAH *stand nude together.*)

RUTH: *(Looking at them naked)* Gawd bless my peeps, 'tis religious art! Hadam 'n' Heve inna Garden a Heden!

MARY: What happent to da snaket?

SARAH: Da serpent hiss 'n' slitheret, 'n' tell lies, 'n' wigglet 'n' flap, 'n' lead all astray.

(*She pries open* DR BROWNE's *mouth and grabs his tongue.*)

SARAH: Here bin da serpent tempter, 'n' now dis picture bin completet. 'Tis time. Ruth. Commencet da rant.

RUTH: *(A prayer)* Dere han't much comfort here tonight, but han't ever been much a dat anywhere, since da world inceptet. What comfort, fellow creatures, they give to da dying Christ? Vinegar sponges 'n' spears.

(There's a delicate penny whistle, unseen, playing a sweet air. All three ranters look up, look at one another, smile. SARAH *nods and* RUTH *Looks at* MARY. *They breathe in unison, loud, twice.* MARY *has a drum, and she strikes two strong beats.* RUTH *begins. As the rant builds in intensity, the three women begin to dance, pulling powerful forces from the earth and raising them into the air. Lights and strange sounds, drums, voices, singing, the quarry engine. Magic is being done.)*

RUTH: I gotta dig,
Gotta dig to da place,
Gotta sink to da place,
To da place a da pain,
To da place a da plain
To da plain a da bone,
To da mouf a complaint,
To da voicet screamet,
To da tongue, to da place,
To da verra verra place,
To da rivah say
NO!
To dis weepet,
Say NO!
To dis sorra,
Say
GAWD, OH GAWD, OH YISROEL 'N' JUDAH!
To da pain 'n' da grief
To da poor da believers
Bya sweat a da Lord

Act Four 83

By da calloused hands a Christ
By da breath, by da blood,
By da bloody tears a Christ
By da wrinkled hands a Mary
'N' da stripet socks a Joseph
'N' DA GLORY HALLEJULAH
'N' DA ANGELS ALLA BLUE!
Like flies dey buzzet
Like da buzzet a da flies
Like da lamb
Like da ram
Like da bitter bite a wine
Like da blood inna mouth
Like da bush inna fire
'N' da curse
'N' da curse
'N' da curse
'N' da curse

MARY: (*Overlaps starting with* RUTH's *"ANGELS ALLA BLUE" above:*)
'N' da earf gonna freezet
'N' da earf gonna crack
'N' da earf go all blacket
'N' da earf
'N' da earf
'N' da watahs a da ocean
'N' da boiling a da sea
'N' da curse, 'n' da hand
'N' da curse, 'n' da dreadet…

(SARAH *has now mounted* DR BROWNE, *riding piggyback, triumphant, as* RUTH *leads him in a small circle.*)

MARY: 'N' DERE GO DA CALLET GLORY!
'N' DERE GO DA CALLET SELAH!
'N' DERE GO DA DEVIL ARMET!
'N' DERE GO DA PITCH 'N' THUNDAH!

'N' da curse bin come
'N' dah curse bin come...

(From Dr Browne's *mouth a wild animal bray—one long raw note. Suddenly from the air above, mighty trumpets play the notes of the* Dies Irae, *E Flat, D, E Flat, C, D, B Flat, C, C. All the other noise ceases,* Dr Browne *slumps to the floor, and the ranters look toward the sound, awestruck. They have ranted many times, and have made magic before, but this is different...)*

Ruth: *(Softly)* 'N' den dere bin a stillet in da passes a da moon...

Sarah: *(Softly)* Selah. Selah. Oh Yisroel 'n' Judah. 'Tis da power a Gawd, oh hallelujah...

(The room is transformed, through lights, into a verdant green bower in a woods.)

Sarah: *(Gentle)* Cross dat stream, fellow creatures, inta dat little woods, bin home...
'N' da leaves sparkle, it bin spring, 'n' tendah, 'n' da light bin silvah, 'n' da tree bark black, 'n' da leaves dat particala shade a green, 'n', Oh, we remembah, 'n', Oh, we be back dere someday, 'n' in dis walk a exile we weepet, 'n' remembah da woods...

(She reaches with great sudden violence toward the heavens. A hot white light, obliterating all other light, breaks down upon her, and upon Dr Browne *at her feet.)*

Sarah: *(Rage)* 'N' pour, let us pour into dis memory, fellow creatures, such...strong...hate.

(All three place their hands on Dr Browne. Dr Browne *shudders and cries. From the fields outside, a deep, ominous earthquake rumble.)*

Sarah: Dat bin enough. 'Tis done, 'n' will unfold in time. Dr Browne, I give you dis, dis one last gift, whatchoo give to my ma: Dat you bin wide awake when da little gentleman come. 'N' he bin coming.

ated Four

(They dress him and lay him back in the bed. SARAH *puts her clothes on.)*

MARY: Nicet rant, Ruth.

RUTH: *(Loading up with silver again)* I bin hinspired. Da curse take, Sarah?

(SARAH *listens. Outside, the rumble rumbles again, fainter.)*

SARAH: Oh, yoop.

(They exit.)

(DR DOGWATER *sneaks in, goes to the Bible, takes out his fake Will, produces a pencil, and speaking as writes:)*

DR DOGWATER: "…and I further stipulate that Dr Dogwater *alone* duh-deliver my eulogy, that nuh-*no* other puh-persons be allowed to suh-speak at my fuh-funeral *particularly* not my uh-overpriced fancy foreign physician whose cuh-cuh-criminal ineptitude in muh-medicinal matters is matched by his guh-guttural Tuh-Teutonically inflected muh-muh-murder of the kuh-king's English."

(He kisses the Will, replaces it, exits.)

(Immediately upon his exit THE ABBESS OF X, *who has been hiding in the curtains, goes to the Bible, and removes* DR DOGWATER's *Will. She takes from her robes a strange-looking device with a crank handle. She inserts the Will in a slot at the top of the device, cranks the handle, and opens a little drawer at the base of the gadget: the Will has been shredded into long strips. She puts the strips back in the Bible, checks under the mattress to makes sure her Will is still there; she kisses it, makes the sign of the cross over her sleeping brother and leaves.* DAME DOROTHY *sneaks out from behind another curtain, replaces* THE ABBESS OF X's *Will under the mattress with her own from the desk, strikes a match, sets* THE ABBESS OF X's *Will afire. She hears someone coming.* DAME DOROTHY *ducks back behind the curtain, dropping the flaming Will, in a panic abandoning*

it on the floor by the bed, smoldering. BABBO *enters, looking for something. Then she spots the tart* DEATH *left on the bed. She claps her hands, picks it up, sticks first one hand and then another hand in the tart and starts to rifle its filling, smearing herself with purple goo. She scratches her head in confusion, then sees* DAME DOROTHY's *Will on the floor.* BABBO *claps her hands again—she's found the Will—she retrieves it and stuffs it in the tart. She begins to leave with the tart, when* DAME DOROTHY *steps out from behind the curtain. She looks on the floor; the Will she dropped is gone. She looks at* BABBO.)

DAME DOROTHY: Where's the…

BABBO: Where da what?

DAME DOROTHY: What's in that tart?

BABBO: *(Hiding the tart behind her back)* Han't see no tart.

DAME DOROTHY: Babbo, give me that tart.

*(*BABBO *bolts from the room.)*

DAME DOROTHY: Babbo! Give me that tart! Babbo!

(She exits in pursuit. DR BROWNE *moans in his sleep; he wakes up.)*

DR BROWNE: Washed. All washed…Up. Unspool, unclench, I will plant this onion in the earth…And go on living…

(He strains to push the blockage out. He is stricken by another searing, tearing pain in his gut. He screams, clutches his side. He opens his eyes again and sees the urn.)

DR BROWNE: You've arrived. Silent urn. Still mouth. I remember the Capuchin catacombs in Rome. That quiet, that fragile stillness. Those dry, deflated bodies. The disappointed faces of the dead.

*(*MACCABBEE *enters with Chicken C, dragging it by its neck; it has swelled even more than when we last saw it—a medicine ball of a chicken; HUGE.)*

Act Four

(HIS SOUL *rises up behind the headboard in silent homicidal expectation.*)

MACCABBEE: Doctah?

DR BROWNE: Go fetch the gravedigger. The urn's arrived.

MACCABBEE: Looket. Da chicken. It bin heavier now dan before. Forty-seven pounds.

DR BROWNE: (*Lying back, closing his eyes*) Monstrous fowl. And what do you conclude, Maccabbee?

MACCABBEE: I conclude dat death been fulla surpriset.

(MACCABBEE *swings the immense heavy chicken back over his head, intending to crush* DR BROWNE *with it; he swings too hard and the force of its parabola carries* MACCABBEE *backward to the floor with a crash.* DR BROWNE *sits up, looks at* MACCABBEE *on the floor.*)

MACCABBEE: Oops. I slippet.

(BABBO *enters.* HIS SOUL *sinks from view.*)

BABBO: Doctah, dere bin someone here ta see you. She wannet me ta prepare ya fer da shock.

DR BROWNE: Maccabbee, go get the gravedigger. Wait. The urn. Unscrew the lid.

(MACCABBEE *does.*)

DR BROWNE: What's inside?

MACCABBEE: (*Head in the urn; his words echo spookily as if being spoken into a deep well [use a microphone]*) Noot but ashy stoof, dead gray sandy grit 'n' bit a bone.

DR BROWNE: From which you conclude?

MACCABBEE: (*Raising his head out of the urn*) Nuffin.

DR BROWNE: (*Quiet despair*) Exactly so. (*Fury*) Where's that gravedigger, you idiot?

MACCABBEE: Inna woods wif yer wife.

(He exits.)

DR BROWNE: Actually, I knew that.

BABBO: Doctah, yer visitah.

DR BROWNE: Is it Alice?

BABBO: How you know dat?

DR BROWNE: I saw her. Has she... Is she some sort of nun?

BABBO: Some sort, but I han't say what.

DR BROWNE: Show her in.

(BABBO exits.)

DR BROWNE: Oh open urn, cough up that dust.

(A spume of dust rises from the urn. DR BROWNE is badly startled, frightened, then:)

DR BROWNE: See? The dead do rise.

(THE ABBESS OF X enters.)

DR BROWNE: *(Finds her presence, the sight of her, frightening)* Alice.

THE ABBESS OF X: You look well, Thomas.

DR BROWNE: *(Attempting politeness)* And you, I must say, look ferocious.
(Almost afraid to ask) Is *he* here, too?

THE ABBESS OF X: Who, Thomas?

DR BROWNE: But no, I suppose he couldn't be.
The silk merchant.

THE ABBESS OF X: *Father?*

DR BROWNE: Does convent life agree with you, Alice? Not too quiet?

THE ABBESS OF X: It is an active order.

Act Four

DR BROWNE:
I'm glad you didn't drown, that's damp.
Into the sea poor Alice was tossed.
Everyone thought that her life was done.
Blankety-blankety she wasn't lost.
She went in a sinner and came out a nun.

THE ABBESS OF X: *(Moving toward the bed)* Thomas, I must talk seriously with you, I—

DR BROWNE: *(Stopping her approach)* The silk merchant Browne. He died... You never knew him, really. He died when I was eight. He was a granite-hearted drunkard, his sheets were soiled and stank like these. Father Dead.

THE ABBESS OF X: Thomas, I need to—

DR BROWNE: *(Turning away from her, trying to stop her from talking, frightened)* My writing desk was once set up facing the window. In the daytime, the view of the fields, the weather and light. But at night, Alice, the window went black, a mirror; I could see nothing in it but my tired face, the little candle light, and sometimes, stranger things. The faces of the dead in the window at night. My children's faces. Father's. Waiting and hungry...I moved the desk to face the wall. Eventually.

THE ABBESS OF X: Is there a Will, Thomas? Where's the Will? He was my father too, some of the money—

DR BROWNE: *(Stopping her)* Alice *(Very fast)* I've had fourteen children with Dorothy; eight died in infancy; those are the ones I love. The others grew large and difficult. I wrote a few books; they knighted me for that, and because I stayed loyal to the king. I was wrong to support him, they were right to chop his head off, progress is inexorable and his blood greased the works. Now I'm dying, and you're a nun, how funny, with many a jolly tale to tell, no doubt, but it's been twenty years and I mourned your death once and

I'm more comfortable now thinking you still dead, so please, whoever you are, go away. Your presence is too vital and it causes pain.

(Pause)

THE ABBESS OF X: *(Placing the vial of holy water on his pillow)* Water from the Vatican—holy water. Do with it what you will.

Some of the money should go to me, Thomas, it was my birthright, too. Father's inheritance.

DR BROWNE: There's a distinctly mercenary scent in the air tonight. This isn't me dying; it's a great deal of money rolling over.

THE ABBESS OF X: *Am I named in the Will?*

DR BROWNE: *(Suddenly desperate) Help me,* Alice. I CAN'T SHIT.

THE ABBESS OF X: Neither could Father, after he took ill. You're fifty years old. So was he. You've inherited everything, even his death.

Good-bye.

(She goes. DR BROWNE *drinks the holy water, greedily.)*

*(*MACCABBEE *enters with a machete.* HIS SOUL *sits up again to watch.* MACCABBEE *sneaks up behind Browne, and then swings the machete mightily back over his head, screaming:)*

MACCABBEE: AAAAAAAAAAAAAAAAAAAAAAAA AAHHH!

(Again swings too hard; the tip of the machete impales itself in the floor behind him. DR BROWNE *looks over at* MACCABBEE, *who fakes a sneeze.)*

MACCABBEE: Choo!

*(*BABBO *enters again.* HIS SOUL *sinks from view.)*

Act Four

BABBO: Secuset da interruptet, but now dere bin another woman ta see you, verra helegant 'n' mystrous. I think she bin foreign; she talket funny.

(DAME DOROTHY *enters*.)

DR BROWNE: Not so foreign after all.

BABBO: No, Doctah, dis han't da foreign woman, dis yer wife.

(BABBO *goes*.)

DAME DOROTHY: Thomas, there's a woman from court come to pay her respects. The wife of the Spanish ambassador. You never told me to expect…

DR BROWNE: Expect anything and everything. Death is full of surprises, right, Maccabbee?

MACCABBEE: Fulla interruptet, too.

DAME DOROTHY: What are you doing with that cleaver?

MACCABBEE: Bin trimmet da shrubbery.

DAME DOROTHY: There's no shrubbery in here.

MACCABBEE: 'Tis good ta be preparet. Ya nevah know where da odd bush pop up. Now secuse me, I gotta go cut da heads offa da rose bushes.

DR BROWNE: Keep your eyes to the ground!

MACCABBEE: Right! Da moles!

DR BROWNE: The moles.

MACCABBEE: Ef I see one, Doctah, I chop it in two.

DR BROWNE: That's the spirit.

(MACCABBEE *goes*.)

DR BROWNE: Where is my Spanish guest?

DAME DOROTHY: I asked her to wait a moment. Thomas, the gravedigger's come…uh, he's *here*. Here's the gravedigger. Mr Pumpkin.

(DAME DOROTHY *opens the door.* PUMPKIN *enters.)*

(BROWNE *glares at* PUMPKIN *a beat, then:)*

DR BROWNE: Oh, good. I can't say I've been looking forward to this, Mr. Pumpkin, but I recognize a grave necessity. Leave us, Dorothy.

DAME DOROTHY: Leave? Why?

DR BROWNE: A man's interment is an intimate matter. Join the others. Search for the Will. I can hear them now, dismantling the library.

DAME DOROTHY: You want to hurt me, Thomas.

DR BROWNE: I used to, very much. And I believe I did, on occassion.

DAME DOROTHY: More than once.

DR BROWNE: I'll be dead. You can remarry.

DAME DOROTHY: I don't care about the Will. I want nothing from you.

DR BROWNE: Then you won't be disappointed.

(DAME DOROTHY *goes.* DR BROWNE *watches her leave and then:)*

DR BROWNE: She's a good person. Too good. No judgment. None at all. I mean, look who she married. See my point?

PUMPKIN: Yes, sir. I do.

(Little pause.)

DR BROWNE: *(Glaring at* PUMPKIN, *trying to make him squirm)* I want to be buried deep. Very deep but... not too deep. Apart from the mob, but not in a lonely place. Avoid the usual clichés—no willow trees, though I'd like a view, for summer evenings. No pine box. Flimsy. Use that urn. Toss out the previous occupant, or better yet, throw me in there with him and let us mingle. *(Little pause)* No markers, or, well, maybe

Act Four

just a little unpretentious stone. Maybe…"Here lies Sir Thomas Browne, scientist." "Here lies Sir Thomas Browne, who made his wife miserable." "Here lies Sir Thomas Browne, no grandchildren…BUT A GENIUS! SHAKESPEARE HAD NOTHING ON HIM!" *(He is now bellowing at* PUMPKIN *with wild hatred and immense pride.)* Or maybe an obelisk! Or a pyramid! A pyre! A *sea* burial, or…*GET OUT OF HERE!*

PUMPKIN: I han't following dis, Dr Browne.

DR BROWNE: *(Great delirious newfound certainty!)* I don't need *you*, wretch! I'M NOT GOING TO DIE. It isn't… *conceivable!* I can't…*IMAGINE* it.
IF I DIE…THE WORLD ENDS! And… *(The certainty is dissipating, the hatred of* PUMPKIN *remains.)* And we'll have no need of gravediggers then.

PUMPKIN: Ef dat happens, Dr Browne, I findet another job. I bin verra…

DR BROWNE: Flexible? Jack of all trades? Descendant of a sturdy race?

PUMPKIN: I bin dat fer sure.

DR BROWNE: Ambitious.

PUMPKIN: Verra.

DR BROWNE: Tell her I died *knowing*.
No, don't tell her anything.
I daresay you'll end up running the whole works one day.

*(*DAME DOROTHY *enters.)*

PUMPKIN: Da works.
Dr Browne. Mrs Browne.
(He strides out, triumphant.)

DR BROWNE: I don't trust that boy, Dorothy. He's tense.

DAME DOROTHY: But dependable.

DR BROWNE: Don't hate me, wife.

DAME DOROTHY: You did not live well upon this earth, Thomas. I never really wanted anything from you. And you leave behind you only a dreadful lot of woe.

(She goes.)

DR BROWNE: *(Considers that for a moment, and then, sadly)* That's probably true.

(DOÑA ESTRELITA *enters carrying a small jeweled casket.*)

DR BROWNE: And what about you? What do you want?

DOÑA ESTRELITA: The English are supposed to be gracious.

DR BROWNE: You're an unexpected participant in these funeral games.

DOÑA ESTRELITA: I bring you trinkets, little toys.

DR BROWNE: Trinkets.
You know me so well. Let me see.

DOÑA ESTRELITA: *(Opening the casket, laying these things one by one in his lap)* Torn scarlet lace.
A rosary.
A dry bit of blackroot.

DR BROWNE: Explain these gifts.

DOÑA ESTRELITA: The scarlet lace. I wore it when I was young, attendant on my husband in the court of King James. The night I saw you for the first time. My weakness for men of learning.

DR BROWNE: The winds that night. Drunkenness. They could barely keep the torches lit, the shutters banged like gunshot, the whole palace groaned.

DOÑA ESTRELITA: The rosary. I prayed for you till the silver beads tarnished black. And after you betrayed me, and fled from the scandal, I prayed for death.

Act Four

DR BROWNE: I prayed too.

DOÑA ESTRELITA: Faint heart, you never had the nerve. The blackroot.

DR BROWNE: Poison.

DOÑA ESTRELITA: Because prayers for death were insufficient…I would have died for you. I bit my hands till they bled. I could have done it but…I survived and went home to Spain. And I have waited ever since…

DR BROWNE: For what? Not for me, the wait's not worth it.

DOÑA ESTRELITA: To wait…for hatred to turn to love again.

DR BROWNE: I thought you'd come on a timber ship. To take me home.

(Pause)

DOÑA ESTRELITA: I have.

(She goes.)

(DR BROWNE watches her go. HIS SOUL sits up and watches her leave as well.)

(MACCABBEE enters, carrying a large goblet of bubbling poison.)

MACCABBEE: You bin live and awake?
Dis is…sumpin da doctah wannetya ta drink. He…uh, he said it bin fer yer cough.

DR BROWNE: *(Facing away from him, deeply sad)* I haven't got a cough.

MACCABBEE: Well, a ounce a prevention…

DR BROWNE: Damn the doctor and his noxious drugs. Set it down somewhere.

MACCABBEE: Ah, come on, Doctah, open yer mouf 'n' I'll pour it in.

DR BROWNE: *(Turning suddenly on* MACCABBEE*) I SAID SET IT DOWN,* YOU NO-NOSE INSUBORDINATE, AND LEAVE ME BE.

(His rage causes another extremely painful intestinal explosion and tearing; Browne screams and clutches his side, holding tight to DOÑA ESTRELITA's *little trinket casket.)*

DR BROWNE: I want peace. All I want is p…

(DR SCHADENFREUDE *and* DR DOGWATER *burst into the room, each with a huge manuscript.)*

DR DOGWATER: *(Placing his manuscript on* DR BROWNE's *chest)* A preliminary duh-draft of my eulogy.

DR SCHADENFREUDE: *(Following suit)* And mine.

DR DOGWATER: Chuh-choose. Muh-my speech affirms the justice of God, the rewards of a luh-life of industry, and your impressive eagerness to enter into Puh-Puh-Paradise.

DR SCHADENFREUDE: Mine's a tastefully humorous recounting of the pathogenesis of your tumor.

DR BROWNE: *(Looking at the manuscripts)* Such massive tomes. How can there possibly be so much to say about death?

DR SCHADENFREUDE: I confess. I've been working on mine for a month.

DR BROWNE: A month! I've only been ill three weeks!

DR SCHADENFREUDE: Call it a hunch…

DR DOGWATER: Now about the state or your, uh, estate…

DR BROWNE: Never fear. Babbo has the Will in safekeeping and will read it to the assembled bereaved after my…

*(*BABBO *enters.)*

BABBO: Secuse me, Dr Browne, but…

Act Four

DR DOGWATER: Y-you have entrusted your Wuh-Will to your cuh-cuh-cuh-*cook*?

DR BROWNE: A trusted family servant. She nursed me when I was a baby. She nursed my father when he was a baby.

BABBO: I nurset yer grandfather too, but he han't bin no babbie, just lonely. He bin da most entertaining of da three.

DR DOGWATER: Buh-buh-buh—

DR BROWNE: Remain calm in the face of adversity, Dogwater. Take your example from me. Maccabbee, show the gentlemen out. Oh, and Schadenfreude. I'm not drinking that potion.

DR SCHADENFREUDE: What potion? I sent no potion.

DR BROWNE: Maccabbee said…

MACCABBEE: Uh, no, I said da doctah sent it, but I han't say which one.

DR DOGWATER: Well I certainly didn't send it.

DR SCHADENFREUDE: Nor I.

MACCABBEE: Right. It bin da other doctah.

DR BROWNE: Another? Good God, there's *another* doctor in this house?

MACCABBEE: A verra famous specialist. He couldn't stay but he droppet da poison…I mean da potion off. Secuse me, Doctah. Dis way, Doctah. Doctah.

(*They file out.*)

DR BROWNE: Babbo, what is that succulent aroma?

BABBO: Da chickens bin broasting like da souls a da damned.

(HIS SOUL *sinks again from view.*)

DR BROWNE: Here, consign these to the flames as well. Kindling.

(He hands Babbo the eulogies. DAME DOROTHY *enters.)*

DAME DOROTHY: Babbo, I apologize for...

BABBO: Da missus pinchet my tart. *(She exits)*

(Pause)

DR BROWNE: No more guests? No more people come to pay their respects, or demand payment, or...

DAME DOROTHY: Only me.

DR BROWNE: I want to be forgiven all my sins, wife. It's very painful, burning.

DAME DOROTHY: There's no burning after, I think it's...a metaphor for something. You look dreadful.

DR BROWNE: I am exceedingly taxed. I am completely terrified, you see.

DAME DOROTHY: I know.
I want to say good-bye, Thomas.

DR BROWNE: No. Not you. No.

DAME DOROTHY: I'll wait with you.

DR BROWNE: For what?

DAME DOROTHY: I don't know, I...

DR BROWNE: For...Death.
I once sat down to write a meditation on Immortality. On the world free of death. Now there's a thought. *Hydriotaphia.* It's my best piece, it's very good, I recommend it. It was at the hanging I first knew, really knew, the possibility of my own death. It was at that trial, when those women were hanged, when they... when it was *my words* that hanged them, I...first knew, then, that I would die, and...

Act Four

Their faces were mottled purple, like plums, waxy. The
wood creaked under the weight of their bodies.
And I hoped to build with golden words a ladder up
to Heaven, and in my final hour I'd remember what I'd
written, and ascend.
(He is getting weaker)
Oh God I am talking myself to death.
Where is my soul? Escaped?
All my life...my words sought paths unknown to me.
Along hidden tributaries they flowed and reached...
unforseen conclusions. The battering complicatedness
of living, it's... And there was no turning back. The
light is always dying.
A fire, wife, I can't see you...

DAME DOROTHY: Here I am, Thomas. You look very far
away.

DR BROWNE: Dorothy, good-bye. The ship embarks at
first wind. The mast and sails are gilded with blood, on
seas of blood we sail, in search of prey. The nets hauled
in by mighty hands, up from the red depths to the
surface, up come the great black nets, full and heavy
with the world's riches, hauled to the stronghold,
to the drybone bank of death, with a hiss and suck
plucked from the waters, in a ruby mist, in a fine red
rain.
You...who must live through this...I pity you...

DAME DOROTHY: Thomas? THOMAS! Oh God,
DOCTOR, DOCTOR!

*(She runs out. HIS SOUL sits up dazedly. DEATH enters,
carrying his knife.)*

DEATH: I've delayed too long; I must accomplish it. I
weep for you, Thomas, this will hurt.

DR BROWNE: Stay away from me, I won't have you
touch me, I'm afraid of you, your knife...

DEATH: I need no tools. *(He drops the knife.)* I have my hands. There is no mystery to this. It's ugly. A simple murder...

DR BROWNE: I gave you my hand once, I was a child, how was I to know what you had in mind, that you'd leave me behind, alone in the forest, not deliver me out of the house of bondage but abandon me here to live in the valley of bones—traitor! Traitor! You never intended to save your boy!

(DEATH places his hands around DR BROWNE's neck.)

DEATH: Let me show you how I love you, child. Words sometimes are not enough. My hands are more expressive.

DR BROWNE: The hands of the silk merchant were delicate hands, used to spooling fine silk thread and not snapping it. I remember a soft caress, once, oh please, PLEASE, release me...*I can't move...*

DEATH: No.
Listen.
The machines in the quarry. Digging deep.
Boom. Booom. Booom. Boooom.

(With each "boom" DEATH tightens his grip on DR BROWNE's throat. DR BROWNE struggles wildly, horrible sounds, and then falls limp. It is violent and ugly. Finally, DR BROWNE is dead. DEATH sighs, picks up the knife, looks at the body. He pries open DR BROWNE's mouth. Removing the Will from his coat pocket, DEATH folds it into a small square, places it inside DR BROWNE's mouth, and then gently pushes his mouth closed.)

DEATH: Thy Will be done.

(DEATH leaves.)

HIS SOUL: Good-bye.

(MACCABBEE rushes in.)

Act Four

MACCABBEE: Doctah? Doctah? WAKE UP!
Ah Christ... He...he bin dead fer real! *(Furious)* He died before I bin able ta kill him!

(HIS SOUL wanders out from behind the bed, almost drunkenly, happy.)

HIS SOUL: *(Looking down, dazed)* Look. I've got LEGS.

MACCABBEE: I tried!

HIS SOUL: *(Looking curiously about the room)* Yeah, yeah...

MACCABBEE: I tried my best!

(HIS SOUL sees the goblet of poison.)

HIS SOUL: I need a drink!

(It goes toward the goblet.)

MACCABBEE: Dat bin a mistaket.

HIS SOUL: *(Picking up the goblet)* Shut up.
(HIS SOUL drinks) Mmmmm.

MACCABBEE: I tried! You saw!

HIS SOUL: Look! Legs!

(It exits toward the kitchen.)

MACCABBEE: BROWNE! YOU DIED TOO SOON! COME BACK! COME BACK!
(He sinks to his knees at the foot of DR BROWNE's bed. Brokenly)
MY NOSE! MY NOSE!

Act Five

POST MORTEM

Black Night, Candlelight

(The bed is stripped, covered in black, the room draped in mourning crepe.)

(HIS SOUL is sitting in a corner of the room, next to a pile of soiled bed linens. It is happily watching, smoking a cigarette and sipping from the goblet of poison.)

(Seated on the bed, BABBO is at work, sewing up the body of DR BROWNE in the shroud.)

BABBO: *(Singing:)*
Dat old monstrah's come 'n' gone
'N' da babbie sleepet.
Dat old monstrah's come 'n' gone
'N' da babbie sleepet.
Dat old monstrah's took his fill;
'N' da babbie sleepet still
Nevah more ta waket.
Nevah more ta waket

(She puts coins on his eyes, gathers up the shroud and, as she finishes the stitching, she tells a story, a bedtime story for a young child.)

BABBO: Oncet upon a time, dere bin an old woman, poor 'n' tired a life, 'n' God curset her wif a babbie though she han't food ta feed herself. 'N' she hiket down to da road, where da poor people trampet, 'n' sits bya side a da road 'n' say:

"Da first one passes by here bin dis kid's godfather, 'n' I han't caret who it bin."

'N' God come strollet by 'n' say, "I wanna be da godfather." But she rejeck God, causet she bin harful mad at him fer cursing her wif da kid inna first place.

'N' den da Devil come by 'n' express simila sentiments, offrin ta be da kid's godfather. But she rejeck da Devil too causet he han't nuffin ta offret except trouble, so she rejeck him.

'N' finally Death come walket by, 'n' he looket like a nightmare, 'n' da sun go blacket where he walk, but da woman light up 'n' say: "You bin da only true friend a mine, you da one thing I can hope fer 'n' know I han't be disappointet inna end."

So Death become da godfather a her kid, 'n' he christen him...Thomas. 'N' da kid growet up ta be a famous doctah wif da power a life 'n' death, 'n' den...

'N' den he died, a course.

(She's finished. She bites off the thread and leaves.)

(DR SCHADENFREUDE and DOÑA ESTRELITA enter stealthily. They pull the body of PUMPKIN's rummy out from under the bed. They place it next to DR BROWNE's corpse on the bed. Then they position themselves to lift DR BROWNE off the bed.)

DR SCHADENFREUDE: Eins, zwei, drei...

(They lift and almost drop him, staggered by the weight.)

DR SCHADENFREUDE: He weighs more than I'd expect.

DOÑA ESTRELITA: He seems to have gotten heavier... Sssssh! Someone's coming!

(They begin running with the body in one direction; DOÑA ESTRELITA stops when she realizes they won't make it out

Act Five

of the room in time. Panicking, they toss Dr Browne's *body back on the bed, where it lands topsy-turvy atop the rummy's body.* Dr Schadenfreude *and* Doña Estrelita *hide.* Babbo *enters.* Babbo *sees the corpses all a-jumble.*)

Babbo: Dat's funny.
Musta slippet.

(*She straightens the bodies out, in the process reversing* Dr Browne *and the rummy's bodies.*)

Babbo: Nicet 'n' neat, dat bin more liket.
(*Sniffs*) Hooh! Sumpin stinket harful a cheap hooch, hope it han't bin me…

(Babbo *starts to leave, then stops, thinks for a moment, turns back to the bed, counts the corpses silently: "One, two." Thinks a moment more, then runs out screaming.*)

(Dr Schadenfreude *and* Doña Estrelita *emerge from their hiding places and start to lift the wrong corpse.*)

Dr Schadenfreude: Do you think he'll fit?

Doña Estrelita: It's a very large oven. Everything reeks dreadfully of rum.

Dr Schadenfreude: (*Indicating the corpse still on the bed*) Our dead ringer must have been a drinker; fortunately Thomas was fastidiously abstemious. It would be infelicitous to introduce a body supersaturated with highly flammable spirits to a roaring oven fire. There could be…an explosion!

Doña Estrelita: Hurry! No time to think!

(*They exit, carrying the rummy's body.* Dr Dogwater *enters.*)

Dr Dogwater: There but for the grace of God go I. We read of well-orchestrated d…d…final days. Like tuh-tightly written dramas. *This*…was not well made.

(THE ABBESS OF X *enters, crosses herself. She sees* DR DOGWATER *and crosses herself again, more ostentatiously.*)

THE ABBESS OF X: The Will?

DR DOGWATER: The uh-ancient cuh-cook has it.

THE ABBESS OF X: *Babbo?* He gave it to Babbo?

DR DOGWATER: Your brother may have lived a genius but he died a loo-lunatic.

(THE ABBESS OF X *leaves.*)

DR DOGWATER: Rah-runs in the family.

(PUMPKIN *enters.*)

PUMPKIN: Pardon me, Pastah.

DR DOGWATER: Cuh-come for him already? We hah-haven't performed the exequies yet.

PUMPKIN: Funeral bin tomorrow. I wannet ta talk to you, Pastah.

DR DOGWATER: Not now, Pah-Pumpkin, I'm too dah-dah-distracted.

PUMPKIN: Bin a matter of business.

DR DOGWATER: I'm listening.

PUMPKIN: I got summat you bin verra interstet ta learn, but I han't gonna tell ya fer free.

DR DOGWATER: What could you possibly know that I—

PUMPKIN: It concernet da quarry. 'N' da Will.

(*Little pause*)

DR DOGWATER: What will it cuh-cost me, this information?

PUMPKIN: Ten shares a da quarry.

DR DOGWATER: Tuh-ten...you must be juh-joking.

PUMPKIN: Small comparet to what it cost you not ta know what I knowet.

DR DOGWATER: Well, nuh-naturally you'd say that but—

THE ABBESS OF X: *(Emerging from the shadows)* Pay it Leviticus.

DR DOGWATER: Uh-eavesdropping?

THE ABBESS OF X: Of course. Does this information concern Dame Dorothy?

PUMPKIN: How you know dat?

DR DOGWATER: Whuh-what could he possibly know about Duh-Dame D...

THE ABBESS OF X: He's her lover.

PUMPKIN: That han't so!

DR DOGWATER: *(Overlapping* PUMPKIN*)* Luh-luh-luh... Uh-*what?*

THE ABBESS OF X: I'm trained to track the scent of carnal sin. You're her lover. Now you have something we want.

DR DOGWATER: Wuh-we?

THE ABBESS OF X: I spoke with Thomas before he died. I'm certain to be named in the Will. Partners. Gloria in Excelsis Deo.
As I was saying. *(To* PUMPKIN*)* You know something we want, and we know something you want kept a secret. So we compromise. Three shares.

PUMPKIN: I han't care ef it bin a secret. 'Tis her worry. Ten shares.

THE ABBESS OF X: Dogwater, what's the local penalty for adultery?

DR DOGWATER: Fuh-fuh-flogging. And thirty days in the stocks for fuh-fuhfornicating.

PUMPKIN: Seven shares.

THE ABBESS OF X: Five.

PUMPKIN: Done
(Produces a document) Sign dis.

(DR DOGWATER *takes the document, reads it, looks at* PUMPKIN.)

DR DOGWATER: Uh-it's already made out for fuh-five shares.

PUMPKIN: *(Producing a pencil)* I bin preparet ta compromise. Sign 'n' I talk.

(DR DOGWATER *signs.* PUMPKIN *takes the document.*)

PUMPKIN: As a fellow shareholder in da Walsingham Quarry I feel it bin my duty ta inform ya dat Dame Dorothy, da soon-ta-be majority shareholder, plans ta—

(DAME DOROTHY *enters.*)

DAME DOROTHY: Plans to what, Mr Pumpkin?
Plans to do what?

(DAME DOROTHY *and* PUMPKIN *look at one another.*)

PUMPKIN: I bin sorry, Dorfy, but you han't listet ta me.

(He shows her the document.)

PUMPKIN: It han't da hentire works, but it bin five shares, 'n' dat's better 'n' nuffin.

DAME DOROTHY: "Nuffin" is precisely what it is.
This man knows nothing of my affairs. He's swindled you.
How could he know my plans?

DR DOGWATER: He...he—

THE ABBESS OF X: ...is your lover.

DAME DOROTHY: Him! He's a commoner!
Hello Alice, I'd heard you'd returned from the dead.

PUMPKIN: I lovet you, Dorfy, but love han't lastet onna small holding farm.

DAME DOROTHY: A commoner and deluded.

THE ABBESS OF X: At the risk of being...indelicate. This afternoon around six I took a little stroll in the woods, Dorothy. There's a lovely clearing with beds of wildflowers.

DAME DOROTHY: Ah.

THE ABBESS OF X: Need I say which two people in this room were making use of those beds? He may not be your lover, Dorothy, but he must be a *very* close friend.

DAME DOROTHY: *(To* PUMPKIN*)* Tell them. I interrupted you.

PUMPKIN: You tell.

DAME DOROTHY: With pleasure.
I plan to close the quarry and give the fields away, back to the people who—

DR DOGWATER: DUH-DO WHAT? YOU PLAN TO DO WHAT?

DAME DOROTHY: Walsingham Fields will be common lands again.

THE ABBESS OF X: Dorothy, that's insane.

DAME DOROTHY: Babbo told me about your visions, Alice. I'd be careful calling other people insane.

DR DOGWATER: This is the fuh-final straw. You're mad, wuh-woman. The cuh-corporation will stop you, you'll be prevented—

THE ABBESS OF X: Sit, down, Leviticus, you're apoplectic.

(DR SCHADENFREUDE *enters.*)

DR SCHADENFREUDE: Ah, my dear Dogwater.

DR DOGWATER: Whuh-where's that Wuh-Will! Where's that Guh-Goddamn cuh-cook?

DOÑA ESTRELITA: *(Entering)* Stay out of the kitchen! I just put a very large roast in the oven!

DR SCHADENFREUDE: And look what I found in the oven fire!
(He displays a charred, smoking, thick manuscript) My eulogy! Yours, I regret to say, I was unable to save…

DR DOGWATER: My eu-eu-eu-eu… *(He runs out)*

DR SCHADENFREUDE: *(As* DR DOGWATER *flees)* I tried my best to pluck it from the inferno, but your prose, alas, is infinitely drier than mine.

PUMPKIN: Dorfy, could we go—

DAME DOROTHY: Mrs Browne, please. Your services won't be required till tomorrow morning. Not at all, in fact. I'll find someone more fit to bury my husband. He was right about you, you are too…tense.

PUMPKIN: As a shareholder I gotta right ta hear da Will readet.

DAME DOROTHY: Then sit in a corner somewhere and please refrain from speaking to me.

(The ranters enter.)

SARAH: We come ta see da houtcome.

RUTH: *(Looking at the corpse)* It look verra satisfactory.

(The rumble in the fields is heard, ominous.)

MARY: Da best bin yet ta comet.

DR DOGWATER: *(Reentering)* Ranters, nuns and foreigners. This place is a fuh-frigging zuh-zoo.

MACCABBEE: *(Entering)* Da cook bin comet.
(He sees HIS SOUL*)* Why hantchoo ascendet?

Act Five

(HIS SOUL *takes a drag on the cigarette, looks at* MACCABBEE, *looks up to Heaven.*)

HIS SOUL: That is a very interesting question. (*Calling out to the audience*) Is there a theologian in the house?
(*It lifts the cup of poison, makes a toasting gesture, and drinks more poison*) To your health, you snoutless procrastinator.

MACCABBEE: Han't rubbet in.

HIS SOUL: I'm famished. I gotta get a bite to eat. (*Exits*)

(BABBO *enters; she's been drinking to fortify her nerves.*)

DR DOGWATER: Well hah-hallelujah! It's the kuh-kuh-queen of Heaven!

BABBO: Thank Gawd, dere bin da correck numba a cadavahs. Musta been delucinatet.

DAME DOROTHY: I think we ought to sing a hymn. In the memory of.

DR SCHADENFREUDE: Hear hear! May I suggest "Oh Mein Gott, Du Rhüst So Denken Geschmecktet Dört die Himmelplatz Abfärht"?

DR DOGWATER: Ah, pluh-please! We'll suh-sing an English hymn. (*To* DR SCHADENFREUDE) *Barbarian.* "There Is a Land of Pure Delight."

BABBO: Oh, dat bin one a my favorites.

DR DOGWATER: Well, anything to puh-please you, Your Guh-Grace. In Memory: Sir Thomas Browne.

THE ABBESS OF X: Requiescat in Pace.

EVERYONE: (*Sings:*)
There is a land of pure delight
Where saints immortal reign.
Infinite day excludes the night
And pleasure banish pain.

There everlasting spring abides,
And never-withering flowers.
Death like a narrow sea divides
This heavenly land from ours.
Amen.

DR DOGWATER: Nuh-now the Will.

THE ABBESS OF X: Read it, Babbo. You have the Will?...

BABBO: Well, I misplacet it, but...

(DR DOGWATER *lunges for the Bible.*)

DR DOGWATER: But here it is!

(*He opens the Bible, and pulls out long shreds of paper.*)

DR DOGWATER: Wuh-what the fuh-fuh-fuh

(THE ABBESS OF X *meanwhile has lunged at the mattress and retrieved the Will hidden there.*)

THE ABBESS OF X: Forget it, Leviticus, the Will of Browne is here!

(*She tears open the seal, as* DR DOGWATER *lunges for the document. There is a brief snarling tug-of-war;* THE ABBESS OF X *wins, doubling* DR DOGWATER *over with a well-placed kick.*)

THE ABBESS OF X: I begin to suspect you *enjoy* this trouncing, Leviticus.

DR DOGWATER: *(Clutching his privates)* I cuh-could get used to it.

THE ABBESS OF X: *(Speed reading through the Will)* AHA! Here! "And all my shares in the Walsingham Quarry I bequeath to my dearly beloved wife Dorothy B—"

(THE ABBESS OF X *instantly starts to rip the Will into shreds.* DAME DOROTHY *rushes to stop her.*)

DAME DOROTHY: What are you...IT TOOK ME TWO-AND-A-HALF HOURS TO WRITE THAT—Oops.

Act Five

THE ABBESS OF X: *(Rushing to the bed)* IT'S A FAKE! WE'LL SEARCH FOR THE—

DAME DOROTHY: If you're looking for *your* version, Alice, here it is.

(DAME DOROTHY *hurls a cloud of black ash in* THE ABBESS OF X'*s face.*)

THE ABBESS OF X: You… You burned it!?!

(THE ABBESS OF X *lunges at* DAME DOROTHY, PUMPKIN *intercedes,* THE ABBESS OF X *flips him head over heels.*)

DAME DOROTHY: Thank you, Alice, you must teach me how that's done.

DR SCHADENFREUDE: Through the Will the dead speak to the living, and Browne remains for once uncharacteristically mum. Through the eulogy the living speak to the dead, and since I am the only one prepared to eulogize the deceased when the king arrives—

DR DOGWATER: *UH-I* am prepared!

DR SCHADENFREUDE: Your eulogy, Doctor, is toast.

DR DOGWATER: *(Triumphantly!)* I have cuh-cuh-committed it to muh-memory!

(*They square off, preparing to duel.* DR DOGWATER *begins, in a singsongy ecclesiastical tenor:*)

DR DOGWATER: "Our Huh-Holy Fuh-Father, who does not suh-suffer us that we should know the hour of our d-departing, nuh-no more that we shuh-should know the duh-destination of our suh-soul on its puh-perilous fuh-final fuh-flight…"

DR SCHADENFREUDE: *(Reading, fast aggressive and loud)* "Honored, esteemed friends and neighbors and fellow citizens of Norfolk, and most especially Your Majesty, before the full auric effulgency and pearline dazzlements of whose presence I am nearly but fortunately not entirely overwhelmed and at a loss of words, confronted with whose Jovian and may I be forgiven for saying it remarkably pleasing and attractive countenance the mere sight of which..."

(They are getting louder and louder, trying to outshout one another.)

DR DOGWATER: *(Continues his speech from above)* "...compared to huh-whose stark and tuh-terrible Ma-ajesty we are as guh-giddy as mayflies, luh-loathsome as eels, wicked and heedless and damnable as vuh-vixen and vultures, lowly and vuh-vomitous as the cah-carrion of the earth; God Almighty in Huh-His infinite muh-mercy has taken fuh-from us our duh-dear Sir Thomas Buh-Browne, and in his puh-parting we should rejoice and make muh-merry, we should cuh-clap our hands and suh-sing hymns of laudation and thuh-thanksgiving, we shuh-should eat ruh-robustly and—"

DR SCHADENFREUDE: *(Continues his speech from above)* "...inspires, conjures, calls forth in me, an inexpressibly grateful recipient for lo these many years of this most exceedingly delightful serene and salubrious island's world-renowned grace and hospitality, the tenderest and yet most thrillingly exalted of memories and recollections of my many many many many years of exquisitely intimate acquaintance with our Sir Thomas Browne, whom I was pleased to call friend, patient, *confidante*, now departed, gone gone gone gone, and yet, with all these memories, we haven't lost him— No! Allow me to share a few dozen of the most select with you. Ah I remember the day we met, it was—"

(The dueling eulogists are toe to toe, shrieking with rage at one another, ready to come to blows, when BABBO blows a shrill whistle. They stop, everyone turns to her.)

BABBO: I got da Will.

Act Five

It bin in da tart. Den da tart disappearet. Den I findet da tart, but da Will han't bin in it. Den I foundet da Will, and I put it back inna tart. And den da missus took it from me, da Will *and* da tart. And den I foundet da Will. *(Little maddening pause)* Not da tart. Just da Will. One lastet time—

DAME DOROTHY: Found it? Where?

BABBO: *(Almost a whisper)* In da doctah's mouth. Aftah he bin dead.

DR DOGWATER: Thuh-then huh-whose...?

THE ABBESS OF X: *(Over* DR DOGWATER's *line above)* Whose Will is it?

(From the urn, a great blast of smoke belches forth!)

(Everyone screams in terror and falls to the floor as, in the doorway leading to the kitchen, DR BROWNE *is standing. He is slim, dressed in dark splendid Restoration clothing, which though not mouldering and decayed, look a bit like* DEATH's *costume.* DR BROWNE *is pale but quite elegant.)*

DR BROWNE: This is the Last Will and Testament of Sir Thomas Browne, Doctor of Norfolk, Author.
(He enters the room.) My will is...to eat. To greedily engorge without restraint and know not eating death. I wake up, I wake up moments after dying—hungry. My life I spent defeating my hunger, I conquered my hunger by eating the world, and yet my hunger will live, it will live on after me, I will *be* hunger. Every gift I ever gave I want to retrieve; every cent I ever paid in tax or wage or purchase I want to steal back; every morsel in the mouth of every child ever fed by food procured with the money I spent I long to snatch back and eat and surfeit and die and disassemble and dust and disappear...
(He considers his corpse on the bed for an instant, and then) And most of all my name, I want to devour! And most

of all, all the words, the words words words! I want to eat my words! Come flooding back to me, my words, unmake the world, the world I made by writing, undo it all, my every word, flood back into my blistered broken mouth and stop it up like clay, forever!
(Pause)
And for all the piddling rest of it, the house, the gold, the quarry... Well of course Dorothy I leave it all to you. To whom else, wife? Companion of my life. I leave everything to you.
(To the rest of them) So much fuss and bother...I suppose it gave the supporting cast something to do. While waiting for the end.

(The rumble from the fields again.)

DR BROWNE: The end has come.
And tell the children, tell my friends, my foes, the future—
NO. Don't tell them ANYTHING

(The notes of the Dies Irae *sound, faintly. From the kitchen, a warm red glow, drifts of smoke.)*

(SARAH sniffs. DR BROWNE, looking at her briefly, also sniffs. Then he sniffs again.)

DR BROWNE: I wonder...what's cooking...in the kitchen?

(He exits through the door from which he entered. Before he disappears from view, he raises his arms. Immediately, a big fiery explosion from the kitchen. A hot red glow in the windows. A very serious fire.)

DAME DOROTHY: A fire, fire in the kitchen!

(She runs out. DR SCHADENFREUDE and DOÑA ESTRELITA look at each other.)

DOÑA ESTRELITA: Perhaps we put the wrong corpse in the oven.

Act Five

DR SCHADENFREUDE: Uh oh!

(DR SCHADENFREUDE and DOÑA ESTRELITA run out.)

DR DOGWATER: *(Looking out the window)* Oh duh-dear, the thatch is catching. The whole west wing is gah-going up.

THE ABBESS OF X: What's that noise?

(The rumbling again, very deep, very low, very loud, and the sounds of mighty whirling winds, and a far-off sound of shouts and screams.)

DR DOGWATER: The ruh-roof caving in, puh-probably.

THE ABBESS OF X: No, another noise, from outside...

(The sounds outside increase, the room grows darker.)

RUTH: Mary, what be dat soundet?

MARY: Soundet like it come from da general direction a da quarry.

DR DOGWATER: The quarry?

(The sound suddenly gets much worse, a terrible, appalling, bone-rattling, theater-shaking, crashing, roaring, imploding sound—the worst sound ever heard, the sound of the world ending. Under it, or over it, the Dies Irae *again. The lights in the candles flicker out as the room grows terribly dark. In the windows a sick green light.)*

DR DOGWATER: Oh my Guh-God!

(THE ABBESS OF X, PUMPKIN and DR DOGWATER rush out. RUTH and MARY follow them. The terrible roaring and imploding continues, on and on. Bits of plaster fall from the ceiling. BABBO and MACCABBEE cower together. SARAH stands, thrilled by the pandemonium, and bows. The sound begins to die, the lights restore.)

BABBO: Dis han't a atmospheret conducive ta grief.

(There is a moist explosion, like something big and wet popping.)

MACCABBEE: Wonder what dat be?

BABBO: It comet from da pantry.

MACCABBEE: Da chicken! Da chicken explodet!

(He runs off. HIS SOUL enters from the kitchen, soot-blackened, smoking a cigarette, carrying a goblet.)

HIS SOUL: *(Ear to the ground)* I hear something. Underground. Tunneling, scurrying, it's...*Moles.* I feel *awful.*

(DOÑA ESTRELITA enters, DR SCHADENFREUDE close behind her. She flings herself on the body of DR BROWNE.)

DOÑA ESTRELITA: Thomas, good-bye, I have failed in my mission!

DR SCHADENFREUDE: Doña!

DOÑA ESTRELITA: What?

DR SCHADENFREUDE: I assume you have connections at court.

DOÑA ESTRELITA: When I am in London the queen and I visit cemeteries together. We make tombstone rubbings.

DR SCHADENFREUDE: The office of king's physician.

DOÑA ESTRELITA: I know a brilliant Norfolk doctor of German extraction who simply *must* be appointed!

DR SCHADENFREUDE: And you, great lady, will receive the ashes of your love, in a small box, by parcel post!

DOÑA ESTRELITA: But how—

DR SCHADENFREUDE: They'll put him in the ground, I'll dig him up. Child's play! I too have an oven...

(DOÑA ESTRELITA kisses DR SCHADENFREUDE, a long hot kiss on the mouth.)

DOÑA ESTRELITA: I must go. My ship departs Brighton at sunrise.

Act Five

(She starts out.)

DR SCHADENFREUDE: Wait!
(He lifts the urn, hands it to her)
A souvenir…

(DOÑA ESTRELITA accepts it and bows. DOÑA ESTRELITA and DR SCHADENFREUDE exit.)

(DAME DOROTHY enters, sooty and disheveled and numbed.)

DAME DOROTHY: Oh. Let it burn, there are far too many rooms in this house anyway. The west wing was where the children lived. It won't be missed.
(She sits on the bed next to DR BROWNE's body.)

(THE ABBESS OF X enters in a big hurry. She says a very fast prayer over the corpse, and then heads out the door.)

BABBO: Where ya headet, Alice?

THE ABBESS OF X: It's a sign from God! Back to France!
(Exits)

BABBO: *(Calling after)* Have a good swim, Alice.

(DR DOGWATER, PUMPKIN, RUTH and MARY enter from outside.)

DR DOGWATER: Bah-bah-bah

PUMPKIN: Da quarry, bin *gone*!

RUTH: Congratulations, Sarah, bin some curse.

PUMPKIN: Da machines…drillet, hit a giant cavern underneaf, 'n'…da ground split, 'n' da whole works just fall right in. Gone. From da rim you han't see da bottom. 'Tis a verra abyss.

SARAH: Gone ta hell.

(The ranters embrace one another.)

RUTH & MARY: Yisroel 'n' Judah!

(The ranters rush outside again.)

DR DOGWATER: The expense, the overhead, it's the end of the wuh-world.

PUMPKIN: 'Tis unfair! My shares bin swallowet! I worket hard fer dem.

DAME DOROTHY: Poor Pumpkin, you always wind up with a pit, in a rut, with a hole in the ground. God beshrew my heart, but I pity you.

PUMPKIN: *(Looking at her hard for a moment, then)* You han't gotta do dat. Dis hurt me sumpin harful but I bin a descendant a a sturdy race. Fuck da countryside. I go to London.
(To DAME DOROTHY *again, with cold hatred)* I han't feel nuffin. *(He exits)*

DR DOGWATER: Y-yes. Not to dah-despair. I've luh-lost everything. *(To* DAME DOROTHY*)* But then again so have yuh-you. Thuh-that's some cuh-comfort. Guh-God moves in mah-mysterious and sometimes ruh-rather malicious ways. To spur us on. And we go on. We duh-dare not do otherwise.

(DR DOGWATER *exits as the ranters return.*)

SARAH: Dorothy.

DAME DOROTHY: I can't rise, I've taken root.

SARAH: Listet, babbie. In ten days dere be a ship sailet from Portsmouth. 'N' me 'n' Mary 'n' Ruth be on it. It sail fer da new world.

MARY: Sail fer America.

RUTH: Dere bin endless land dere, belonget ta no one. Only savages.

MARY: We maket a community dere, a fellow creatures.

SARAH: Da new world, Dorothy. Bin you comet?

(DAME DOROTHY *stands slowly.*)

DAME DOROTHY: First I have to bury my husband.

Act Five

SARAH: Portsmouth. Da ship bin callet *Circe*. Circe bin a Greek witch.

(The ranters go.)

HIS SOUL: *(Sings:)*
Happily I turn the earth,
tunneling for all I'm worth.
Who needs Heaven, who needs souls?
Below is Paradise for moles...

DAME DOROTHY: Good-bye, husband. We've populated the earth. We'll have our grandchildren, never fear, the children were only waiting for you to go. And generations will descend, down through the centuries, cursed by our gold, Browne upon Browne.
I'll go my solitary way to America, and maybe I'll marry again. I'll bring only one possession:
(She holds up a slender, elegant book, reads from the title page) "Hydriotaphia or Urne-Buriall," by Sir Thomas Browne. I'll read it to children to help them fall asleep at night. Your words. To turn into pure music in their heads as they dream.
(She kisses the corpse's forehead and leaves.)

HIS SOUL: *(Sings:)*
Heaven's bright and full of fluff,
And never is there dirt enough,
So Heaven's not where moles are found
But digging deeper
Deeper deeper
Always deeper underground...
(Speaking, looking over the audience, the room, the theater with great wonder and awe and joy) My goodness. So *this* is what the earth is like. So this is what a *body* is. So this is what people are. It's been *quite* an experience.
(Holding up goblet) And this concoction is delicious! And these *cigarettes*, well, *yum yum*, I recommend

cigarettes to every —Um. Urk. (*A violent spasm of the gut*) Uh oh.

(*Another spasm*)

This is anticlimactic, don't you think? Oh, well.

(HIS SOUL *dies, collapsing in the pile of soiled laundry. A faint, distant, solemn single church bell chimes.*)

MACCABBEE: (*Entering*) My nose! Lookit! Lookit at my nose! Tell me I han't been dreamet!

BABBO: It han't bronzet no more!

MACCABBEE: Resurrectet! A fleshly proboscis as in days a yore!

BABBO: Praise Gawd! It been a mackerel!

MACCABBEE: Verra! Chicken C! It burstet! 'N' inside dere bin maggots! 'N' da maggots sproutet wings, 'n' dey bin flies! 'N' da flies growet black 'n'gold, 'n' turnet inta bees! 'N' da bees maket honey, clover honey, 'n' honey cover da walls, run on da floor, sweet honey, smella clover, fields in flower, 'n' I accosted myself, "Maccabbee," I says, "draw a long deep breath a dis miracleous perfume!" 'N' I drawet, 'n' den... Outta dat dead metal comet dis livet protuberance! Alive, alive, 'tis verra nice indeed.

(*He inhales. She inhales.*)

BABBO: Dat laundry reeket. Tomorrow we burnet.

MACCABBEE: Dere bin good smells 'n' bad, 'n' eiver one gets me going.

(*They look at each other.*)

BABBO: You wanna?

MACCABBEE: (*Looking at His Soul*) Poor babbie.
Poor Dr Browne. God bless his soul.

BABBO: Hamen.

MACCABBEE: I wanna.

BABBO: Mordal sin. It bin a long, long day.
(They come together as lights go to black and...)

DA VERRA END

AN AFTERWORD

When HYDRIOTAPHIA was in preparation at Berkeley Rep, with rehearsal time severely limited, I wrote a series of sketchy suggestions for Jonathan Hadary to consider while constructing his Browne. Jonathan greeted the pages I'd prepared with a wonderfully weary and slightly incredulous smile, accepting them graciously, promising to read them; actors know how to handle a control freak. I knew better than to ever ask if he had read them. A magnificent actor, Jonathan made Browne entirely his own.

It's a tricky part, Dr Browne is, and the entire extended farce relies very heavily, in terms of sustained tension and antic forward motion, on the performance of the title role. Publishing these notes is a risky and problematic decision. I don't mean to suggest that there is only one way the good Doctor can be played. But the notes might be a useful guide for an actor or director who is beginning to think about the part, and perhaps non-actors and non-directors will find them illuminating vis-à-vis the performance aspects of the text.

Some General Thoughts about Browne:

Stephen Spinella, for whom the part of Browne was written, watched Bette Davis movies in preparation; one great queen learning from another, the waspishness and the wit. He even modeled his hair and makeup ever so subtly after Bette's. For whatever it's worth…

Heinrich Heine, the great nineteenth century German-Jewish poet, in horrific pain for *eight years* in his bed in Paris, was apparently all through his ordeal a dazzling conversationalist whose voice betrayed nothing of his torment, and even though he almost never slept he wrote over a thousand magnificent poems from his bed.

Browne's a writer and he loves words.

He's very very very afraid of dying, and of Death.

Everything internal he shares with his audience.

When others are onstage, if he wants them to be in the room he greedily engages with them. Otherwise, he tries various stratagems to expel them. He almost never ignores anyone. All his life he has been observing and watching and thinking about what he watches and observes.

He's appalled by the way others treat him and the way they treat the fact of his incipient demise—from Babbo's discussion of the funeral food to Dogwater's carping about the Will, he is aghast. Their matter-of-fact acceptance, even in some cases their eagerness for his death, wounds and shocks him.

He has a good sense of humor.

His body has failed him but his mind is alert. There is rarely grogginess or weakness. His body is simply swollen, toxic, useless. The head is wide awake. What is killing him is his guts exploding.

He frequently turns on a dime, emotionally.

He never relaxes! He is active, his mind is working fast, even frantically, either to try to save himself, to distract

An Afterword

himself from his terror and pain, or to meet his death head-on by shoving people away and facing being alone with his terror and pain.

None of these actions work—he is *always* returned to the fact he states at the top of the play: "I will die today."

Act One

Browne wakes up, immediately wide awake, into terror, knowing that something frightening (Death's first appearance) has just occurred.

He instantly calls for his comfort—Maccabbee—to ascertain if this morning is his birthday. It is—and he knows that he will die today.

The fear that realization engenders sets his busy mind to work. He wants to see the gravedigger—he wants to see the man who is fucking his wife.

The screaming at his wife makes his belly hurt, badly, for a moment. ("I shouldn't scream, it brings on the bloating.") Babbo's questions about the food pull him out of the pain, her fondness for him ("...such a fussy 'n' patricula man.") calms him a little and he tells her about the dream he has had the previous night.

The dream is painted by him (the writer!) in quick sure simple strokes, a harsh little poem. I may be dying but I can still do this! And do it well!

This cheers him a little—enough to engage with her joke. ("There should be tears!")

The quarry engines call to him. He loves them; he loves what he owns, what he has made, his world ("*My* engines!") —and HE DOES NOT WANT TO DIE.

Schadenfreude comes in—Browne believes his leeches will help. The treatment almost kills him. He passes out.

While unconscious: he dreams that the gravedigger is screwing his wife. And then he dreams about moles. The moles are dark, beautiful, sexy and frightening. He dreams about the urn, also frightening, and inviting.

He wakes up: Dogwater's yelling blasts him wide awake, instantly out of sleep and scrambling to locate himself—"Am I dead?"—and when he realizes (instantly!) that he's still alive, he immediately assesses and deals with the menace of the moles; demanding of his wife that she fetch the gravedigger, he looks for the urn.

It annoys him that Dogwater is here, and that he's intruding, he knows what Dogwater wants. He decides to torture Dogwater a little, pretending not to know him (he pretends successfully, we don't need to know that it's pretending), putting him in his place with his credentials ("I studied in Padua…"), and as always with his ability to dazzle with words ("Unearth the urn…").

And as always the words take him to the truth—that he is going to die. And that he cannot face dying. ("It is impossible to CONCLUDE *anything*.")

He abandons the game with Dogwater. It offends him that Dogwater is demanding a look at his Will. They don't love him, the pastor only wants the money to be secured, and his wife is only interested in inheriting it and marrying the gravedigger. He decides to deny that he has written one. He wants to watch them writhe.

Having hooked them, he dismisses them.

He gives the Will to Babbo to hide, the only person he trusts.

His Soul, which has been noisily berating him more and more in the past week, demands that he let her go—that he die. He would like to believe that she is the

An Afterword

best part of him and if he releases, if he dies, she will ascend and he will live in Eternity. But he is afraid to die, and like everyone else, she doesn't love him, she only wants something from him; he decides to refuse her as well. He listens for his quarry engines, their love song to him, and he lets them lull him to sleep, escaping her demand.

While unconscious: asleep, he dreams of a timber ship. Someone is on the ship, though he cannot see who it is. The ship frightens him. He squirms a bit in fear.

He wakes up: Ruth's "EARFEN CLOT" wakes him in two stages—eyes closed, he sits up, seeing the scary timber ship on the cold river.

His eyes pop open—he is wide awake. And alone. And scared. He calls for company—His Soul—let's argue some more! But it's gone. He is frightened by its disappearance. He tries to reassure himself by saying, as any rational person would, that it doesn't exist: "Losing you is less than losing nothing..." To distract himself from the fear, to be alone no longer, he calls for the comforting presence of a manservant.

Browne orders the chicken experiment.

This begins as a distraction but he as usual is led by his mind to a search for the truth—that he really wants to know whether the soul exists, whether it has substance, as His Soul now seems to have. He is used to using Maccabbee to think these things through; Maccabbee makes him explain and that helps clarify— he has always known himself to be too impulsive and quick.

But he hears himself distracting himself ("You're right. It is...nuts."), and remembers what is REALLY frightening here—dying. ("Why is there no one here to comfort me?") He is embarrassed that he's reduced to asking this clod for company, revealing so much of himself...

So Browne sends Macc away.

But he's lonely and frightened, he changes his mind, calls Maccabbee back. The moles, the menace, do something about it, kill the bastards. ("A mixture of cyanide and boiling lye...")

He hears himself again, and again angrily sends Maccabbee away, making sure as he leaves that he's going to do the experiment (This sort of moment is what Estrelita is referring to when she says, "You are split in two..."), because Browne really needs to know...

AND HERE—he has a spasm of pain. He feels things giving inside. He tries to metaphoricize it (to control it): "The ropes on the dock are slipping from the moorings, and I'm...off..." ANOTHER SPASM OF PAIN—and he's out.

A moment (Macc's little speech: "Fetch da rottet birds.") and he is suddenly jolted awake by a third SPASM which is so severe it knocks him out cold.

While unconscious (this corresponds to Death's and the Abbess's entrances toward the end of the Act): he dreams a terrible terrible dream. His dead father is in the room with a huge kitchen knife: when Browne was a child his father used it when drunk to menace his mother, and him.

He is so frightened by this vision that he decides to flee the room by letting His Soul go—by dying. ("Into your hands I...COMMEND MY...") And there it is, eagerly awaiting his demise, which pisses him off, and frightens him; he changes "commend" into "condemn" and decides to wake up instead, and when he does, to his horror, confronts his dead sister (GASP!) and dead father! (GASP!) This cannot be ("NO!").

And they go away.

An Afterword

He is now fully awake: Dorothy and Dogwater rush in. He asks if this can have been real. He's sure he saw them. The sight of his father is by leagues the most terrifying thing he's ever seen. In the midst of his terror, the ship returns as an image to him—but it's a different ship, another ship, not the coffin ship, but… some vessel bringing love. He looks for and finds his quarry engines' love song. Again, he lets them lull him to sleep, leaving a last little poem in the air, a talisman to protect him while he sleeps, protect him from terrible Father Dead.

While unconscious: he sleeps, dreaming of the ship, solace, protection.

Act Two

Browne begins to wake at Babbo's, "DON'T DIE, DOC-TAH…"

He has been dreaming of rescue, love, warmth on the timber ship. He feels happy calm and peaceful. Someone who loves him has come for him. He has been very cold and he asks for warmth, which he gets from her.

Then she leaves. ("The sun…") He is cold again. He opens his eyes ("…clouds over…").

And he wakes up into a nightmare—terrible Father Dead is back. He hides under the covers, completely abjectly terror-stricken.

It works! He is still terrified ("I cannot see that face again."), but there was comfort for him in the room just a moment ago—a Spanish Lady…?

His Soul is back, furious as ever; but Browne has just triumphed over Death (by hiding from him) and is determined to triumph over it too, denying its existence ("You're not my soul, either, just some malcontented noisy thing…"), straining to shit out the tumor, and when he can't do that— telling her that everything he has is his and his alone—he will not comply with its request—he won't give up anything ("It's all mine..."). Everything has been created by his desire and his intellect and none of it belongs to anyone else.

His Soul reminds him that the writing was a collaboration. He has considerable pride in what he has accomplished ("I recorded it for posterity!"), but His Soul reminds him how immensely beautiful and clean and pure and holy its song was, and he knows that what he wrote was none of those things: his words took him to places he didn't anticipate, to a darkness and meaninglessness at the center of existence, to a void.

That's what is in the three ellipses, in Act One ("The baby in the...the genesis of things."), here in Act Two ("When I described what I saw inside, the room had changed, it...was rather empty, and") and in Act Four ("The battering complicatedness of living, it's..."), it's a very human place, where opposites coexist and overwhelm and intoxicate and affright—and for which no words exist—which is why this place, this ellipsis, draws him in and frightens him so...Browne can describe everything but he cannot describe that. It is a dark and bitter realization, a dark and bitter place, and the fact that he is actually rather fascinated by it makes it only worse, he feels ashamed, alarmed...

Browne feels he should be pitied rather than despised for this. ("Pity me! You should! The world made me, the word betrayed me, I never wanted to see...")

So that when Maccabbee comes back in, Browne is in a very troubled place; he feels that he has failed God, who sent him this beautiful song, which he then smudged and besmirched, simply by being flawed, greedy, fearful—human.

An Afterword 133

He doesn't want to deal with Maccabbee. At first he has no idea what Macc's talking about, strangling chickens—and when he remembers the experiment it seems like a pathetic joke, incredibly ridiculous considering what he's just realized, his failure, his shame. He wants this torment to end ("...let's end this farce...").

But as always when he arrives at Death's doorstep, ready to face it, he finds he can't. ("What were the results?")

And Browne is alarmed to hear that the results are something unexpected—the unknown, the weirdness, that really scares him, really makes mock of his attempts to control this day. WHAT IS GOING ON HERE!? ("IT CANNOT CONCEIVABLY WEIGH *MORE* DEAD THAN...")

This connects to what he says in Act Four, and it's at the heart of the terror— ("It isn't possible! I can't conceive it!") —that there is something in this dying business that he with all his intellect cannot control.

And then just as he is getting really frantic and scared, this death portent, the Weaver of Shrouds, appears, and in trying to get away from her, and this terrible fear, and this room, to physically get away, he causes something in his swollen gut to rip. He tries to deal with this physical crisis, and with the frightening weaver, and in the midst of all this Father Dead appears, and Browne curls away from him into a little ball at the uppermost corner of the bed—hiding worked once before, and he has to calm this fire in his gut—and calls/begs for the psalm. The psalm reassures him, he takes a peek and sees Death has gone...

The doctor arrives, unfortunately the wrong one.

During the prayers he takes inventory of his innards: he realizes that he has done some serious damage to himself and that as he said at the beginning of the day, he is, in fact, going to die, and soon. He is as he says "working on it."

Dogwater comes at Browne demanding the Will. Browne doesn't want to give it to him, he is frightened, he wants to live, he tries to get some distraction action going by talking about/railing against his children, attacking Dorothy, keeping Dogwater at bay—he makes a last stab at hanging on, roaring.

But as always his words lead him back to death, bitterness, regret. ("He used to send copies to me, but then he...stopped.") Dorothy's, "You got what you wanted," is painful to hear. He is returned to the bad place—while the doctors fight and Dogwater storms off—and perhaps even Dogwater's, "This is what comes of you irresponsibility," gets to Browne. He makes a decision, the net result of all that has happened so far: he decides he is ready to end it.

This is a big change: though there will be moments when he thinks otherwise, from this point on for the rest of the play Browne is trying to face dying, he is trying to die.

He asks to go to the river, which he knows will finish him off—he makes the request first of Schadenfreude, then of Dorothy. Browne tries to get out of bed on his own power; unable to do that, he asks the weaver.

Even though this is his last request, as he says, even though he has resolved to go, no one will help.

Then help arrives. The woman from the ship. It is astonishing, a miracle, an unexpected occurrence that is for a change favorable, reassuring.

An Afterword

While she talks to Schadenfreude, Browne watches her closely and realizes who she is. It's a private realization, the audience doesn't need to see it, but probably it comes here. By the time Browne asks her, "How did I know you were coming to me?" he knows who she is.

When he says, "How mysterious," he is referring to her astonishing arrival at just this juncture. There is real grief and regret in, "I think now I never thought enough about love." Here is a mystery Browne didn't plumb deeply enough, and now it's really too late.

And then he goes off to the river.

At the River: the washing is extremely lovely, though he is unconscious for most of it.

Act Three

Asleep while being bathed, dried, carried back from the river to the house: in his dream the moles have changed into something quite sexy and wonderful, full of mystery and delight.

He half-wakes: Dogwater's yelling brings him up to the surface waking, and he tries to describe vast twisty enticing tunnels under the river, full of moles—and even half-awake Browne composes poems, this one about moles, their blindness seeming deep and full of powerful meaning—blind perhaps like a seer, or a prophet, tragic and yet deep diggers, like Browne himself, nosing through the earth for the truth.

There is groggy joy in making the poem.

Act Four

During the Rant: the lovely warmth and ease and caress of the bath is banished in the rant. All the things Browne regrets and is ashamed of, all his terror of dying is called forth in this nightmare, ending with a premonition of the hunger that comes after—this is when, during the rant, he cries.

He wakes up: Dorothy's, "BABBO!" wakes him, and again he wakes into terror, alone.

After he tries to shit, he has a spasm—what ripped intestinely in Act Two is worsening. Browne realizes that he is in trouble, nearing the end.

The urn has arrived, a death portent, silent, still…

He is terrified still of dying, he remembers the Capuchin Catacombs in Rome, how sad and disappointed those faces were, how horrible…

Maccabbee enters. Browne sends him to get the gravedigger—unfinished business. Babbo arrives to tell him Alice is here. ("She wannet me ta prepare ya fer da shock.") He is very much afraid to see her, he calls Maccabbee back to delay that moment, and also to tell him what it looks like, inside that urn…

It's as bad as Browne thought. All delays lead him back to the fear. Maccabbee's no use—and here Browne decides to face these terrible tasks, Alice, the gravedigger, dying…Browne sends Maccabbee away.

He tries to prepare for the shock of seeing Alice, asking Babbo what she's like. Babbo goes to fetch her, leaving Browne alone for a moment with the urn.

He tries to control the fear of it, of that stillmouth, by making a little epigram, a little poem line, an apostrophe. ("Oh open urn…")

An unexpected and scary surprise. The spume of dust. Browne freaks a little, he tries a little joke… ("See? The dead do rise.")

And Alice is in.

She frightens Browne, and her resurrection suggests that scarier people still may have returned.

An Afterword

He dispenses with the formalities ("You look ferocious..."), and asks what's really worrying him ("Is *he* [father] here, too?"). Browne tries to reassure himself ("But no, I suppose he couldn't be."), but it's too menacing and that face was too real ("The silk merchant.").

Her incredulity offends and frightens Browne—he doesn't want to be going mad, seeing things. So he tries a little pleasant exchange ("Does convent life agree with you, Alice? Not too quiet?").

Even composing a little ditty for her ("...Into the sea poor Alice was tossed...") as he did when Alice and he were children.

But she's still there, *wanting* something. It's too terrifying. He begins worrying about the silk merchant again, and he talks to silence her voice, to not listen to this demanding... *But* talking about the silk merchant makes Browne remember that he is as his father was when he died.

Alice talks again. Browne turns away from her, he tells her about the writing desk and how the faces of the dead terrify him, how *her* face is terrifying to him.

And still she won't go. She too wants the Will. Browne decides to evict her.

He tells her everything there is to tell about himself, beginning with his wife (who is getting all the money), and ends by telling Alice that she is hurting him, explicitly asking her to go ("Your presence is too vital and it causes pain.").

It enrages Browne that Alice won't leave after he tells her this, that she is still after the one thing she came to get, the Will, the money. He blasts her ("There's a distinctly mercenary scent...").

It works, she starts to leave, but Browne is afraid. Can she help him?

She can't and doesn't.

She leaves. Maybe the holy water will help, so he drinks it.

Babbo announces the arrival of a foreigner, and Browne knows who it is. He expects Estrelita, but Dorothy enters. He finds her presence reassuring ("Not so foreign after all."). After all is said and done, Browne knows his wife and she knows him.

Maccabbee too reassures him, familiar. Browne gives Macc his marching orders, sends him off, and prepares to meet the next visitor who has come to say good-bye—Estrelita.

But Dorothy tells Browne she's brought the gravedigger. This is a betrayal. But also what he asked for. He attacks her with considerable nastiness, in front of Pumpkin, and after she flees, Browne feels badly, he even admits to his misbehavior in front of this upstart, this usurper, and the usurper throws down a gauntlet. ("Yes, sir. I do.")

Browne realizes that Pumpkin's ready to fight. Browne chooses to fight by giving Pumpkin this list of impossible contradictory orders: do this, but not that! This, and not that! Browne uses the words, the surprising twists, the paradoxes of the speech about burial to stab at him; he becomes flush with the victory, which he imagines his verbal dexterity, his talent, is giving him. He flings false modesty at Pumpkin, he flings his sins at Pumpkin ("...who made his wife miserable..."), his failure to have grandchildren—BUT (a hairpin turn) HE IS A GENIUS! SHAKESPEARE HAD NOTHING ON HIM! He deserves AN OBELISK! A PYRAMID! A PYRE! A GRAND SEA BURIAL...

An Afterword

HE IS THE CENTER OF THE UNIVERSE, and he cannot die! The idea is preposterous! Everything, even this wretch, depends on him and his continued life! He will never die. He dismisses the possibility, and for a moment feels immortal, victorious ("We'll have no need of gravediggers then!").

But as soon as Pumpkin starts to talk back, and even worse, to walk, healthy, young...Browne can only hope to hurt Dorothy through Pumpkin by saying, "Tell her I died *knowing*." He wants her to know that she hurt him terribly.

And then he takes that back. There are several meanings to: "No, don't tell her anything."—leave her with nothing, just silence, leave them all with that, or possibly Browne has decided not to hurt her; or possibly he means both.

Estrelita's visit is painful, and also redemptive: she has loved him all this time, in spite of his having been a coward, of his having abandond her, all things Browne has spent his life despising himself for. She never stopped loving him, and she promises to take him home with her.

Estrelita's visit completes the stations Browne has had to visit on his way to what he believes is a truce he's made with dying. The last interruption of the eulogies is dispensed with easily, with magisterial calm—he wants to be alone, with Dorothy, to try to face the end.

They are embarrassed to be together. He is moved by her loyalty, she is frightened that he is clearly near the end; they are sad that there is so much hatred between them, her betrayal of him, his cruelty to her. He confesses to his role in the killing of the women accused of witchcraft—the memory of their hanging has never left him; the guilt he has suffered, he who is essentially a decent man, has been an awful torment.

He drifts, slowly letting go, the toxins inside overwhelming him. He has a final vision ("Dorothy, good-bye. The ship embarks at first wind. The mast and sails are gilded with blood..."), which is also his farewell to the world, his final poem. She loses her nerve at the end, and cannot wait to watch him breathe his last; she runs away to find help, and Father Death finally makes his move. Browne begs for his life, tries to move this monster to pity, tries reproaches, pleas, but...

BOOM BOOM BOOM.

Act Five

When Browne comes back from the Other Side to deliver his Will, he is hungry, vibrant, joyous, mobile, feeling great for the first time in years. He is also an instrument of Vengeance, and is enjoying that, the delivering of Justice, immensely.

www.ingramcontent.com/pod-product-compliance
Lightning Source LLC
Chambersburg PA
CBHW060156050426
42446CB00013B/2860